WILTSHIRE COOKERY

GOOD CHEER

Beefe, mutton and pork, shred pies of the best,
Pig, veal, goose, and capon, and turkey well drest;
Cheese, apples and nuts, jolly carols to hear,
As then in the country is counted good cheer

WILTSHIRE
COOKERY

ANGELA RAWSON &
NIKKI KEDGE

Illustrations by Angela Rawson

THE DOVECOTE PRESS

First published in 1984 by The Dovecote Press Ltd
Stanbridge, Wimborne, Dorset

ISBN 0 946159 24 6

Designed by Humphrey Stone
Photoset by Characters, Chard, Somerset
Printed and bound by Biddles Ltd
Guildford and Kings Lynn

CONTENTS

ACKNOWLEDGEMENTS

For their generosity and help with many of the recipes we would like to thank: Mrs Joan Stevens, Mrs Mary Roberts, the residents of Abbey House, Malmesbury, Mrs Jane Grigson, Major and Mrs Gibbs, William Tullberg, Mr Gilbert Mills, Mrs Madge Townsend, The Wiltshire Archeological and Natural History Society, and Wendy Williams, Chief Technical Manager, St Ivel Ltd.

INTRODUCTION

Wiltshire's cooking is inevitably a reflection of its landscape and the way of life of those who live in it. The distribution of soil types, of woodlands, downland and rivers, of high ground and low, have determined what can be farmed in the county. Most foods are eaten throughout Britain, a few remain linked to a particular town or area. In Wiltshire's case, the sheep traditionally fattened on Salisbury Plain, the dairy vales in the north, and the 19th century development of the bacon-curing trade have provided many of the recipes in this book.

Food and diet have changed dramatically over the past hundred years, and many of the ingredients we take for granted when cooking were once. only enjoyed by the rich. In 1838, Wiltshire was reckoned amongst the poorest counties in England. The farm labourer and his family then lived mainly on potatoes and turnips, supplemented by bread, cheese and bacon fat. The land on which he worked may have yielded beef, ham, mutton, poultry and grain, but little of it appeared on his plate. Most of it was taken to market, and as canals were dug and roads improved, an increasing amount of Wiltshire produce found its way to the cities. The arrival of the railway accelerated the process, but at the same time it opened up massive new markets and inspired a gradual improvement in agricultural conditions. For the trade was two-way. The train that left Wiltshire laden with bacon and Bradenham hams returned with cheaper sugar and tea, as well as new and better quality varieties of fruit and vegetables.

In some ways Wiltshire is almost two counties. The saying 'as different as chalk and cheese' originated in the contrast between the north and south. The chalkland of the south was sheep and corn country, whereas the rich pastures to the north were renowned for their dairies, producing the once famous but now extinct North Wiltshire Loaf Cheese. The differences in soil and topography were at the heart of the distinction, but they spilled over in a whole variety of ways. Beer, for example, was the main drink in the south where good malting barley was grown, whilst in the claylands of the north cider was the staple drink. The north was the stronghold of the family farmer who produced cheese, butter, eggs and milk on his own land, and consequently enjoyed a better diet than the shepherd tending his flock on the Plain. The differences even shaped the character of the people. Because the northern farmer had to rely on fluctuating harvests and varying markets for his produce, he seemed to develop a more turbulent and rebellious character than his southern neighbour.

Such differences were probably not apparent in the days when the people from the outlying villages crowded into Wiltshire's town to attend the weekly and monthly markets. We can still get some idea as to what was sold in those medieval markets from the street names and the many butter and cheese crosses in the county. Salisbury, for instance, has a wealth of rows and lanes commemorating the produce sold there in the past: Fish Row, Ox Row, Salt Lane, Oatmeal Row, Cook's Row. Poultry Cross is the only survivor of the city's four market crosses. Its companions were a Wool Cross in New Canal, Barnard's Cross – the site of the first cattle market, and a Cheese Cross which once stood at the western end of the market near the site of the present library.

Salisbury's commercial prosperity was founded on wool and corn. Vast flocks of sheep once grazed the surrounding downland, making Wilton mutton the standard local fare. Yet gradually the flocks dwindled. In the early-19th century, stimulated by the Napoleonic Wars, the widespread enclosure of land led a decline in both corn and sheep farming – a decline, in the case of corn, that was not halted until the downs were ploughed and sown to feed the nation during the Second World War.

In contrast, the 19th century saw the north of the county prosper through the trade in liquid milk, a trade made possible by the excellent connections between the dairy country and

London. The bacon-curing industry also grew, thanks to the Harris family who took the initiative by buying Irish pigs from the large droves that rested at Calne on the journey from Bristol to London. The pig also played a part in the economics of dairy farming by consuming the whey and providing manure for the hay meadows and small areas of arable. Many cottagers kept their own pigs, adding to its importance as a source of revenue. So valuable was the pig that it came to be described as 'the gentleman who paid the rent. You can use everything but its squeak.'

The game recipes we have included owe their origin to the many large estates scattered throughout Wiltshire. Except for the rabbit and pigeon, they were once cooked only for the gentry, but are now widely available. Indeed, the ingredients for many of the recipes can now be bought anywhere in England. But there is a taste of Wiltshire in all of them. Their ingredients can be farmed, grown or freshly picked in the county, some include its name in theirs, and all without exception are a tribute to the skill and inventiveness of many generations of Wiltshire cooks.

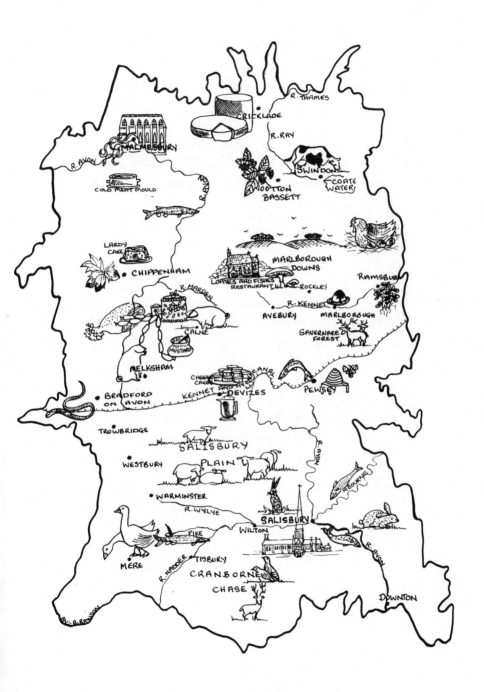

R.THAMES
CRICKLADE
R.RAY
MALMESBURY
R.AVON
SWINDON
COATE
WATERS
COLD MEAT MOULD
WOOTTON
BASSETT
LARDY
CAKE
MARLBOROUGH
DOWNS
CHIPPENHAM
LOAVES AND FISHES
RESTAURANT
ROCKLEY
RAMSBURY
R.MARDEN
R.KENNET
CALNE
AVEBURY
MARLBOROUGH
MUSTARD
SAVERNAKE
FOREST
MELKSHAM
CHEESE
CAKE
CANAL
BRADFORD
ON AVON
KENNET AND AVON
DEVIZES
PEWSEY
TROWBRIDGE
SALISBURY
WESTBURY
PLAIN
WARMINSTER
R.WYLYE
R.BOURNE
SALISBURY
PIKE
WILTON
R.AVON
MERE
R.NADDER
TISBURY
CRANBORNE
CHASE
DOWNTON

All the recipes are for eight healthy appetites
unless otherwise stated. In virtually all cases the quantities
can be reduced where necessary.

SOUPS

Apple and Walnut Soup

Despite the length of time it takes for the walnut tree to begin cropping, at least one was often planted in farm orchards or the garden of country houses. We were lucky enough to have a walnut tree in the grounds of our previous restaurant at Wootton Bassett. To store walnuts, take off the green outer covering and store in layers of dry sand. Beware, gloves must be worn as the green covering stains fingers and anything else it may be allowed to come into contact with.

1 lb cooking apples
2 oz walnuts, shelled
½ pint milk
½ pint strong chicken stock
¼ pint double cream
2 teaspoons curry paste
2 large onions
Small carton natural yoghurt
2 oz butter
1 oz plain flour
2 teaspoons chopped tarragon (or 1 teaspoon dried,
though fresh is best)
1 dessert-spoon caster sugar
A little whipped cream for serving, and a few chopped walnuts

Scald the milk and pour over the walnuts; leave to infuse. Peel and chop the onions and apples. Melt the butter in a saucepan, cook the apple and onion in the butter until soft. Mix the flour with a little milk and mix to a smooth paste until it resembles single cream, then add to the milk and walnut infusion. Pour the chicken stock onto the apple and onion.

Add the milk and walnuts. Stir in the curry paste, tarragon and sugar. Cook gently for 30 minutes. Allow to cool a little.

Liquidize the soup and strain through a fine sieve into a clean saucepan. Heat this gently, do not boil. Add the cream and yoghurt, cook for a few moments. Serve with the whipped cream and chopped walnuts swirled on top of the soup. A little curry paste can be added to the cream if desired.

Beetroot and Garlic Soup

The beetroot has been with us since the Middle Ages. It has a wonderful earthy taste and when made into a soup the tainting of other foods by its purple juice is avoided. This soup is a lovely, delicate creamy-pink colour and can be served either hot or cold.

1½ lbs cooked, peeled beetroot
1 crushed clove garlic
¼ pint single cream
1½ pints strong chicken stock
4 medium sized cooked potatoes
2 medium sized onions, peeled and chopped
3 oz unsalted butter
1 bay leaf
salt and black pepper
Parsley, chopped for the garnishing

Peel the garlic and crush with a little salt. Melt the butter in a large pan and sauté the onion and garlic until the onion is soft but not brown. Chop the cooked beetroot and potatoes, add them to the pan. Pour on the stock, add the bay leaf, season and simmer for ½ hour. After the half hour, remove the bay leaf, allow the soup to cool then liquidize until smooth. Add most of the cream, leaving a little to swirl on the top of the soup when serving. Do not boil. Top with the chopped parsley and serve with wholemeal bread.

Eel and Parsley Soup

The abundance of eels in Wiltshire's rivers made them traditionally cheap to buy. There are many ways of serving them; eel pie, jellied eels, smoked eels, and in soup – the recipe given here. Ask your fishmonger to skin and prepare the eels and cook them as soon as you can, the flesh soon deteriorates.

SERVES SIX

1 lb small eels
1 pint fish stock (chicken or veal could be substituted)
Small piece of lemon rind free from pith
1 pint water
10 whole black peppercorns
Salt
2 oz unsalted butter
3 tablespoons plain flour
2 large onions, peeled and chopped
Bouquet garni
2 egg yolks, beaten
1/2 pint milk
1/4 teaspoon sugar
4 tablespoons finely chopped parsley
1/4 teaspoon ground mace

Put water, stock, mace, lemon rind, bouquet garni and peppercorns into a large saucepan. Season with the salt, bring to the boil and add the eels, simmer for 20-30 minutes until the eels are tender with the flesh coming away from the bone. Strain off and set aside the liquid, discard the bouquet garni, lemon rind and peppercorns. Remove the eel meat from the bones and cut into pieces 1 inch long.

Heat the butter in the cleaned saucepan and cook the onion over a low heat for 15 minutes until soft and transparent. Stir in the flour and add the cooking liquid gradually, add the milk, stir continuously until the soup comes to the boil, has thickened and and is smooth. Add the eel pieces and simmer for 3 minutes.

[5]

Blend about 3 tablespoons of the soup with the beaten egg yolks, add this to the soup with the sugar and stir over a low heat for 2 minutes. Do not let it boil or it will curdle. Stir in the parsley, check seasoning, serve at once with chunks of wholemeal bread.

GIPSYUN AT STOUNHENGE

Zo wen tha day wur drawin ni,
There wur zich fussen mang the maids,
A meakin zich girt pies an cakes,
Ta want we wur naï bit afraid.

A gir big piece of beef they'd cook'd,
An zich a woppin ha had bought,
They wur obliged ta cut un droo,
Ta get un in the biggest pot.

★ ★

Zo Fan did spread a girt big cloth
Apon tha grass, an we zat down,
An mead shart wirk of beef an ham,
Vor appetites we ael ad voun.

An we did ate and drink za long,
Till nothin skierce wur left bit bounes,
Then we got up ta look about,
An zee tha girt big hanshint* stounes.

*Hanshint (ancient)

Wiltshire Rhymes, Edward Slow

Eltrot Soup (Wild Parsnip)

Eltrot is an old Wiltshire word for the wild parsnip which can still be found on waste ground and grassy places. The roots should be washed, peeled and boiled until quite soft, about ¾ hour, then mashed and pressed through a sieve to remove the fibrous parts. The purée makes excellent cakes by mixing with flour, butter, spices and frying. Whether wild or cultivated, the young and freshly pulled parsnip has the best flavour and is the most tender.

6 small parsnips
2 large onions
1 clove garlic
3 teaspoons good curry paste
3 oz unsalted butter
2 pints chicken stock
¼ pint single cream
Salt and black pepper

Peel and slice the parsnips and onion. Peel the garlic and crush with a little salt to form a paste. Melt the butter over a moderate heat, add the parsnips and onion, cover, and cook until the vegetables are soft. Add the garlic, curry paste, chicken stock, salt and pepper and simmer for 20 minutes.

Liquidize the soup, check the seasoning and add the cream. Reheat gently, do not boil or the soup will curdle. Serve with hot wholemeal bread.

Game and Chestnut Soup

Pheasant or pigeon are probably the best choices for this soup, for the scarcity, and cost, of the other game birds make them worthy of more special attention. This is a delicious and filling soup, and goes well with wholemeal malt bread.

1 small game bird (cooked)
2 large onions, peeled and chopped
1 large carrot, chopped
4 sticks celery, chopped
4 oz mushrooms, sliced
1 lb tomatoes, skins removed
1 lb shelled chestnuts
1 pint strong beef stock
1 oz beef dripping
2 teaspoons tomato purée
Salt and ground black pepper
Grated nutmeg
1 bay leaf
1 tablespoon redcurrant jelly
¼ pint red wine
3 tablespoons medium sherry

Remove the meat from the bird, chop into small cubes, put to one side. Into a large saucepan put the carcass of the bird, stock, ½ pint of water, the bay leaf, carrot, ½ the quantity of onion and ½ quantity of celery. Simmer very slowly to get all the flavour from the carcass. A little more water may need to be added if the liquid reduces too much. After two hours take the stock from the heat and pour through a strainer into a measuring jug, you should have around 1 pint of stock.

Melt the dripping in a clean pan, then add the remainder of the chopped onion and celery, cook until soft. Roughly chop the tomatoes, add these to the pan. Also add the mushrooms, chestnuts, stock and red wine. Cook for 20 minutes. Allow to cool then liquidize to a purée. Put the purée back into the saucepan.

Add the seasonings, redcurrant jelly, nutmeg, sherry and tomato purée. Stir well. If the soup is too thick for your taste, add a little extra water or stock. Heat through until hot but not boiling. Finally add the chopped meat and serve with hot crusty bread.

Tomato and Orange Soup

Reading from surviving 18th and 19th century household accounts, the wealthy could afford a more varied diet by the addition of imported luxury items such as oranges, lemons and spices: all of which are now widely available. This soup is very visual in its rich orange colour, especially when served in white soup bowls with a swirl of cream and chopped basil as a garnish.

2 oz tomato purée
3 lb skinned, seeded tomatoes
3 oranges
1 medium onion, peeled and finely chopped
1 pint chicken stock
2 oz unsalted butter
2 oz plain flour
1 small clove garlic
1 teaspoon sugar
Salt and black pepper

Melt the butter in a pan and add the chopped onion and carrot. Cook lightly. Add the flour and stir well. Cook for 5 minutes. Continue stirring. Add the tomato purée, chicken stock, and the juice and zest of the 3 oranges. Cook until smooth and glossy.

Next, add the tomatoes and season with the garlic crushed with a little salt, sugar, salt and pepper. Simmer for 30 minutes.

Liquidize the soup, then pass through a strainer. Return to the heat, adjust the seasoning if necessary. Serve with a whirl of double cream in the centre of each portion and chopped basil if you are lucky enough to have any.

Marlborough Sheep Fair Day 'Soup'

The final event in the farming year on the Marlborough Downs was the large sheep fair held in the middle of September. Thousands of sheep would be driven to the fair, some travelling many miles before reaching the fair field which would be thronging with shepherds and farmers, all eager to buy or sell their sheep at the best price. All this would be accompanied by the never ending din of baas, barks, and shouting from the auctioneer.

This 'soup' is really a thin type of very economical casserole and was often eaten by the shepherd and his family on arriving home after the fair was over. The recipe comes from J. A. Leete's *Wiltshire Miscellany* and was made by the sheepkeeping community on the Marlborough Downs.

½ lb lean mutton or lamb (from neck, shoulder or leg)
2 onions sliced or a handful of spring onions using the green
2 cups of peas
1 cup shredded lettuce
1 cup of water
salt and pepper

Cut the meat into small pieces. Put into a pan with the peas, sliced onion and lettuce, add water, salt and pepper. Bring to the boil and cook very gently until the meat is tender (about an hour). Add extra rich stock but do not make too liquid. Turn into a hot dish or tureen and serve with boiled potatoes, home-made bread or brown rice.

COTTAGE IDEAS

'Passing by the kitchen door, I heard Louisa, the maid, chanting to a child on her knee.

Fether stole th' Paason's sheep;
A merry Christmas we shall keep;
We shall have both mutton and beef –
(but we won't say nothing about it).'

Field and Hedgerow, Richard Jefferies

A shepherd on Salisbury Plain in 1901.

Cream of Artichoke Soup

Jerusalem artichokes were first grown in England on the Hampshire Downs and were a great novelty in 1617 when first served as a vegetable. It would not have taken long for them to have travelled over the border into Wiltshire. A Dr Tobias Venner, physician to the ill and frail at Bath, tried them and found them too strong to recommend as a cure, for they were a 'provoker of wind and caused torment to the belly'. The artichoke is a delicious vegetable however, and is often requested in our restaurant. It also makes an excellent hedge; we have two in our garden screening the lane, the slender, large leaved stalks growing to about 5 feet making wonderful cover, and in the autumn the tubers provide soup and vegetables.

2 lb Jerusalem artichokes
2 large onions
3 oz unsalted butter
1½ oz unsalted butter for the roux
2½ fluid oz strong white stock (chicken or turkey)
½ pint double cream
pinch of salt
salt and black pepper
1½ oz plain flour

Peel and slice the artichokes and the onions. Melt the 3 oz of butter in a large saucepan, add the artichokes and onion, cook until soft. Add 1 pint of the stock and simmer for ½ hour. Liquidize the stock and artichokes to a purée, push the purée through a sieve to remove any lumps. Take the 1½ oz of butter and the flour, cook together in a saucepan for a few minutes until the roux takes on a beige colour, stir all the time. Add the purée to the roux a little at a time. When all has been well mixed add to the rest of the stock. Season to taste and add the pinch of sugar to bring out the flavour. Cook the completed soup until well blended. Add the cream. The soup must not boil once the cream has been added.

Wiltshire's three main rivers are its two Avons (Bristol in the west and Hampshire in the south) and the Thames. But the greatest attraction for anglers are its many chalk streams, virtually all of which provide the fast running water required by trout and grayling. The Nadder was once renowned for its catches of grayling, and the Kennet has been famed for its trout since the 17th century. Thanks to its hatches of May-fly, large numbers of big, strong fish are still taken from the river, particularly at Littlecote and Chilton Foliat. Elizabeth I regularly breakfasted on Ebble trout when staying at Wilton House, as did Charles I – who esteemed the trout above all other freshwater fish. Sadly, salmon are rare on the Upper Hampshire Avon, but their numbers have increased in recent years between Salisbury and Christchurch.

Despite the abundance of the trout, Wiltshire's rivers have their fair share of coarse fish. Tench, pike, dace and carp are caught in both Avons. In *The Natural History of Wiltshire*, John Aubrey described the eels at Marlborough as 'incomparable; silver eeles, truly almost as good as trout'. Aubrey also mentions a small lamprey eel, 'lamprills', as being taken from the Avon at Malmesbury. Crayfish were once plentiful at Salisbury, as well as at Ramsbury and in the Avon at Chippenham. Freshwater crayfish are now a luxury, as are the lobster that used to be carried in creels on packhorses into Salisbury and sold in the Market.

River Trout with Anchovies and Mint

River trout and mint are a natural combination, both – so to speak – being inhabitants of the same element. The wild water mint grows by the edges of streams, damp meadows and woods. There were many women herb gatherers in John Aubrey's day, especially around the village of Minty, where there was an 'abundance of wild mint, from whence the village is denominated'. The combination of flavours make this a very tasty dish and a welcome change from the inevitable almonds. It is best to make the slit along the back of the trout, not the belly as this method stops the filling from falling out. You make the slit as close to the backbone as possible, starting from the head, first one side then the other, working carefully down to the tail. Ease out the backbone and the tail and discard. The head can stay on or off according to preference.

TO SERVE FOUR

4 fresh trout, gutted and cleaned
Salt and black pepper to taste
Large bunch of chopped mint
1 teaspoon ground nutmeg
4 oz browned breadcrumbs
4 oz melted, unsalted butter
4 anchovy fillets, mashed
Butter unsalted for cooking the trout

Cook the anchovy fillets lightly in the butter, reserve the butter to pour over the trout when cooked. Mix all the ingredients in a bowl, including the cooked anchovies. Stuff the mixture into each trout, place in a pan and fry in the butter for 4 minutes each side until slightly browned on the skin. Pour the anchovy butter over the trout and serve with a fresh green salad.

Trout Mousse with a Watercress Mayonnaise

Watercress is cultivated in the clear, even flowing trout streams, the beds being renovated each year in the early autumn when the cress has been harvested. On account of having to stand in water for many hours, labour in planting out the beds was once difficult to obtain and those who worked them were quite often afflicted with rheumatism.

Watercress beds in Wiltshire were once prolific, Ramsbury and Pewsey having beds, and at Bishopstone the cress was in great demand for the markets of Birmingham, Manchester and London.

1 lb trout, poached, skin and bones removed
¼ pint of milk
½ pint of the poaching liquid
3 level tablespoons plain flour
1 sprig fresh fennel or dill, chopped
1 tablespoon anchovy essence
2 teaspoons tomato purée
Juice of ½ lemon
1 tablespoon of medium sherry
½ oz gelatine
4 tablespoons warm water
½ pint of mayonnaise
2 bunches of watercress
Salt and black pepper
¼ pint double cream

Mash the fish until smooth. Melt the butter in a saucepan, add the flour and cook for 3 minutes stirring all the time. Remove the pan from the heat and add the poaching liquid and the milk gradually beating in each addition. Add the chopped herb, anchovy essence, tomato purée, sherry, lemon juice and the seasonings. Dissolve the gelatine in warm water and add to the hot sauce. Put to one side and allow to cool.

When the sauce is beginning to set, fold in the trout meat. Beat the cream and fold into the trout mixture. Put the mousse into individual pots or one large dish, and leave in a cool place until set.

Wash and trim the watercress, reserve a few sprigs for decoration and steam the remainder for 10 minutes. Rinse under cold water and liquidize or chop it finely. Add the watercress to the mayonnaise and blend in well.

Decorate the trout mousse with twists of cucumber and lemon peel, with a sprig of fresh fennel or dill. Serve with the watercress mayonnaise and thinly sliced brown bread and butter.

Trout in Oatmeal with Crispy Bacon

This simple trout dish makes a welcome change for breakfast. If we have a busy day and know that we are not going to have time for lunch, this is one of the dishes that we have for breakfast – accompanied by lots of hot toast, home-made marmalade and a jug of freshly ground coffee.

TO SERVE FOUR

4 one pound trout
2 eggs, beaten
Porridge oats with bran
8 rashers of bacon (2 per trout)
Vegetable oil for cooking

Have the fishmonger fillet the trout if not already filleted. Dip the fillets into the beaten egg, then into the oats to cover the fish. Fry the bacon in a little of the oil until crisp, keep hot. Add a little more vegetable oil to the pan and fry the trout for 3 minutes on each side. Serve at once with the bacon chopped and sprinkled over.

Devilled Pike

In the days when it was necessary to poach to break the monotony of bread, cheese and potatoes, a fresh pike would have made a welcome change of diet. A still, sunny day was required for poaching pike, usually in early spring, for too many ripples made it impossible to spot the fish. A long, thin ash or hazel stick with a wire noose at one end was the only tool required. Pike lie motionless in the water and can be wired easily if done carefully. Once the wire noose was past the fins a quick jerk and the pike was on the bank. You can of course, for this recipe, substitute any white fish, but if using pike it is best to remove as many bones as possible.

TO SERVE FOUR

1½ lbs pike (or other white fish)
4 tablespoons olive oil
2 tablespoons flour
6 fl oz tarragon vinegar
4 tablespoons clear honey
1 clove garlic, crushed with a little salt
1 small onion, peeled and chopped
½ teaspoon ground mace
Salt and black pepper to taste
1 good teaspoon curry paste

To fillet the pike cut off the head with a sharp knife, slit along the belly and clean it well. Reserve the roe as they are delicious and the size of caviare. Spread the fish apart, turn the fish back up and press all along the backbone until you feel it give, turn the fish over and pick out the backbone. Scrape the fillets away from the skin, the flesh comes away quite easily. Cut the fish into chunks and dust them in the flour. Fry in the oil until crisp and brown. Put the fish pieces into a saucepan and cover with the honey, vinegar, crushed garlic, curry paste and mace. Season well and simmer for 15 minutes. Serve with brown rice and a green salad.

[18]

To Cook a Salmon or Trout

Clean the fish if not already cleaned. Fill the stomach cavity with a large sprig of fennel, parsley and a bay leaf, a few knobs of butter, salt and ground black pepper, and the juice of 1 lemon. Line a roasting tin with a large sheet of tin foil and place the fish in the centre, pour over a large glass of white wine. Wrap the fish tightly in the foil; do this well to prevent any of the liquid escaping. Wrap again in another piece of foil and fold over the seams tightly. Try to get as much air out of the 'parcel' as possible.

Fill a large fish kettle or suitable container deep enough to cover the 'parcel' with water; simmer gently until cooking time is up (allow 10 minutes to the pound). When cooked, lift the fish out of the pan, unfold the foil and allow to cool a little before removing the fish skin using a sharp knife to avoid tearing the skin and flesh. If you wish this dish to be a cold one, leave the fish in the foil with its juices after skinning, this will keep your fish moist.

The skin is much easier to remove when the fish is warm.

Lobster

Lobster is not immediately obvious as being synonymous with Wiltshire, but a letter from Jane Austen to Cassandra Austen on Friday 17th May 1799, written from Bath, confirms that Wiltshire, or at least Devizes could provide lobsters, possibly from Bristol.

'At Devizes we had comfortable rooms and a good dinner, to which we sat down about lobster, which made me wish for you, and some cheesecakes, on which the children made so delightful a supper as to endear the town of Devizes to them for a long time'.

This recipe is taken from Mrs Beeton's *The Book of Household Management* 1859, and is one which Jane Austen might well have eaten.

1 Lobster
4 tablespoons white stock
2 tablespoons double cream
Pounded mace and cayenne pepper to taste
Breadcrumbs

Pick the meat from the shell, and cut into small square pieces; put the stock, cream and seasonings into a pan, add the lobster meat and let it simmer for 6 minutes. Serve it in the shell, which must have been nicely cleaned, and have a border of puff pastry; cover it with breadcrumbs, place small pieces of butter over it and brown before the fire (under the grill). Serve with a green salad and a chilled bottle of Sancerre or Muscadet.

LIGHT LUNCH OR
SUPPER DISHES

North Wiltshire Cheese

Dairy farming used to be the mainstay of agriculture in North Wiltshire, the fattening of cattle, sheep and pigs were all ancillary to it. North Wiltshire cheese is sadly no longer made in the county. The milk for these cheeses came from longhorn cows, the most popular bread at that time. In 1798 5,000 tons of North Wilts cheese was produced, averaging 4½-5 cwt per cow.

Wiltshire cheese was a hard pressed, close textured cheese similar to Double Gloucester. It was made as a 'thin' 16 lbs cheese or a 'thick' cheese, 30-40 lbs in weight. Both were flat and cylindrical. It was also made as a loaf or truckle, 5-12 lbs in weight, and it was this that became known as the North Wiltshire cheese.

Communal cheesemaking was popular in Wiltshire, whereby many herds were driven to a central cheesemaking farm. This meant that the milk was at the correct temperature and did not have to be heated, enabling the cheese to be made twice a day. There would of course have been many variations on the basic recipe as each farm would have had its own method.

The Wiltshire County Council Cheese School at Whitley Farm was making in 1893 a Wiltshire Cheese. This particular recipe was known as 'Mrs Vines' method, Mrs Vines presumably being a cheesemaker at the farm.

The required amount of milk was heated to 96°F and one measure of annatoo added to every hundredweight of cheese. This gives the pale orange colour. Rennet was added as much as would coagulate the milk and an hour later one teacupful of 'cheese spice' per hundredweight of cheese. This spice was dissolved in one quart of warm water and was obtained from Messrs. Neale of Chippenham. The curd was cut very small, the curds and whey stirred up for several minutes and then covered to keep warm. Later the curd was scalded to 96°C, then pitched for 15 minutes, after which the whey was carefully dipped off. This scalding was not done for the North Wilts cheese and was consequently moister, softer and flakier in texture. The curd was cut three times, ground, salted and vatted. It was pressed for 15 minutes, then each cheese broken through the middle, turned into the vat in a dry cloth and process repeated (excluding the breaking) at night. The following three days the cheese was rubbed with salt and each time returned to press. Finally, it was pressed for two days in a Holland cloth (cheese bandage) and then left to dry on shelves, being turned daily.

Cheese Savoury

This simple savoury is a great favourite, especially when unexpected guests drop in. You can use almost any cheese that you have in the larder at the time, though a strong cheese gives perhaps the best flavour. We use Cheddar or Double Gloucester and if you can use home-made wholemeal bread it will improve the dish enormously.

Any grated cheese of your choice
Double cream
Unsliced bread for thick toast
Butter for the toast

Grease a fireproof dish and put in enough cream to cover the bottom; add a layer of grated cheese.

Make some thick toast, butter, and cut into fingers. Lay them onto the grated cheese. Add another layer of cream then a top layer of cheese. Put into a hot oven for 10 minutes. Eat at once.

Cheese Ramekins

Rummaging through a pile of ancient cookery books in a second hand book shop in Salisbury we came across a very dilapidated, coverless book. All trace of the original author had disappeared. A loose page fluttered to the floor and reading between the old tea or coffee stains we found this recipe dated 1736. We have added the chopped Wiltshire ham to make it a little more interesting.

2 eggs
12 round rolls
½ lb grated cheese, Cheddar
½ lb Double Gloucester cheese
4 tablespoons unsalted butter
4 oz lean, chopped Wiltshire ham
Pepper to taste

Mix the ham and the grated cheeses together, add the pepper and the butter. Beat the eggs well then add them to the cheese and butter mix. Blend well together.

Cut the rolls in half and scoop out the centre, fill each half with the cheese mixture. Place the filled rolls onto a baking tray and bake in a hot oven 400°F (200°C), gas mark 6, for 20 minutes. They will rise to twice their original size. Eat as soon as they are ready taking care not to burn your mouth.

Chilled Ham Mousse

This easy to make mousse is ideal as a first course or a main dish with salad. It is also excellent for picnics. Chicken, cooked and minced, can be substituted if there is no ham available.

12 oz minced, cooked ham
¼ pint aspic jelly
¼ pint béchamel sauce
3 tablespoons mayonnaise
½ pint whipping cream
1 teaspoon chopped fresh tarragon (the French variety has
more flavour than the Russian)
Slices of cucumber and strips of lemon rind for garnish

Line a mould or small individual moulds with a little melted aspic jelly and allow to set. Decorate the bottom of the mould with the lemon rind and cucumber, pieces of tarragon leaf can also be used. Spoon a little more jelly over the garnish and allow to set. Mix the ham, béchamel sauce, mayonnaise and the spoonful of tarragon, stir this well, then add the remainder of the aspic jelly.

When the mixture is on the point of setting, fold in the whipped whipping cream, turn the mixture into the mould or moulds. When the mousse has set, dip the mould quickly into hot water to loosen the mousse, turn the mould over onto a dish and lift off the mould. Garnish with a little more lemon and cucumber if desired.

The Truffle

The truffle is to be found (though it is now very rare) on the light chalklands of the downs of Wiltshire as well as those of Hampshire and Kent. The truffles were sniffed out by dogs. In Wiltshire the pack being a mixed breed of Russian and French poodle. The season was between late September and March, and the trufflles were at their best just before Christmas when they were fully grown and their scent was at their strongest.

If you would like to search for this irregular potato shaped fungus, it is to be found buried near Beech trees about two to four inches down. They have a nutty taste and a sweet smell. There is supposed to be a yellow fly that is a tell-tale sign that there are truffles under a certain tree.

Should you be lucky enough to find a fresh truffle, brush off the soil, slice thinly and sauté in butter. You can, if you wish, then serve them in a puff pastry case. Alternatively, after brushing them clean preserve in fat, cognac or madeira.

Most truffles today are commercially canned, a process which shrinks them to half their original size. The taste of the canned truffle is usually the best that cooks can do, but its dark, contrasting colour makes it good value for the extra touch that it adds to the visual effect of patés, cold mousses etc.

Thomas Yeates truffle-hunting near Winterslow in 1910.

Egg Mousse

We are fortunate with our supply of eggs as they come from the free range Wellsummer Cross hens bred by Mrs Ann Peutherer at the end of Rockley Lane. This dish can either be for a first course, light lunch or supper served with a fresh green salad and wholemeal bread.

7 hard boiled eggs (reserve 1 for garnish)
1 pint double cream
3 teaspoons gelatine
¼ teaspoon paprika (optional)
a little Worcestershire sauce to taste
a little anchovy essence
salt and black pepper

Separate the egg yolks from the whites when the eggs have cooled. Pass the yolks through a sieve then chop the whites finely. Mix the yolks with the whites. Whip the cream and add the egg mixture, mix well and add the salt, pepper, anchovy and Worcestershire sauce.

Dissolve the gelatine by putting it into a small bowl which is placed over a little hot water in a saucepan. Put this over a medium heat until the gelatine is dissolved. Add to the egg mixture, blend in well. If you have one, use a dark coloured bowl for the mousse as this enhances the colour. Slice the remaining egg into rings and place around the top of the mousse. A few rings of cucumber may also be used as garnishing, as can fresh sprigs of parsley. Serve with thinly sliced brown bread if eaten as a first course.

Mumbled Eggs

Mumbled is an old fashioned word for scrambled. This simple breakfast dish can be made more interesting by adding chopped, smoked Wiltshire bacon or a few pieces of anchovy. With the addition of smoked salmon, it becomes a first course for a lunch or dinner party. To make more attractive place upon a round of hot toast and decorate with sprigs of fresh parsley.

TO SERVE FOUR

4 eggs
2 oz unsalted butter
Pinch of salt
Ground black pepper
Unsliced bread for hot toast

Put the butter and salt into a saucepan and heat over a moderate flame. Break the eggs into the butter and stir gently all the time until a change is seen in the mixture which tends to solidify. Before the mixture becomes too thick, remove from the heat still stirring. Spread it upon thick buttered toast with a few turns of the pepper mill sprinkled over the top, or place into a serving dish which has been previously warmed. This dish must not be over cooked as the eggs will become hard and spoil.

Wiltshire Bacon Scones

These scones make a delicious alternative to bread, served hot from the oven and spread thickly with butter at breakfast or tea time, or for lunch accompanied by a freshly-tossed mixed green salad.

4 sticks celery, chopped
1 onion peeled and grated
4 oz rindless, smoked bacon
1 lb self raising flour
¼ teaspoon salt
Black pepper
2 tablespoons chopped parsley
1 egg
Scant ½ pint milk
½ teaspoon mustard powder
2 oz dripping

Put the chopped bacon into a frying pan and fry for a couple of minutes, add the grated onion and chopped celery, fry for 5 minutes then allow to cool.

Sift together the flour, mustard powder, salt and pepper, rub in the dripping and rub together until it resembles fine bread-crumbs. Add the parsley and stir in the bacon and vegetables.

Beat together the milk and egg then stir it into the flour. Knead the dough on a lightly floured surface. Grease a baking tray, shape the dough on the tray into a round, mark into eight sections lightly with a knife.

Bake for 25 minutes in a hot oven 400°F (200°C), gas mark 6.

'Undoubtedly the most famous smuggling story of Wiltshire relates to the wily moonrakers of Bishops Cannings who completely fooled two excise officers one moonlit night. The excisemen came upon the smugglers in the act of retrieving some kegs of brandy from a pond where they had been dumped for safety earlier in the day.

As the men skimmed the water with their hayrakes the officers stopped to ask what they were doing, only to be told by the men that they were after 'thic gurt yaller cheese'. The officers pondered for a moment and then laughed derisively as they spotted the moon's reflection on the water. They rode off pitying the poor half wits who were trying so hard to pull it from the pond. As soon as the officers were safely out of sight the real booty was raked to the surface, and it was the smugglers who burst out laughing.'

Tales of Old Wiltshire, Cecilia Millsom.

Fresh Peaches with Stilton Dressing

'To watch the peach, nestling in the warm nook, day by day deepening its delicate hues under the loving touches of the greatest of all artists, the Sun'. That is how Richard Jefferies described this delicious fruit in *Landscape and Labour*. The Stilton dressing that accompanies the peach always amazes and delights our guests when eaten as a first course in our restaurant. It is requested time and time again throughout the summer months coupled with appeals for the recipe, so here it is.

4 large ripe peaches
(these must be fresh as tinned peaches will not go
with the dressing)
Lettuce heart

FOR THE DRESSING
4 oz mature Stilton
¼ pint single cream
1 teaspoon cider vinegar
¼ teaspoon salt
2 turns of the pepper mill
½ teaspoon caster sugar
A little milk

Finely grate the Stilton into a bowl, put the Stilton, cream, vinegar, salt, pepper and sugar into a liquidizer and blend together on a medium speed until evenly mixed. Take care not to over-liquidize or the mixture will become too thick. If this should happen, mix in a little of the milk to loosen the sauce. A thick coating consistency is required. Pour the completed sauce into a bowl and cover until required.

To peel the peaches, place the fruit in a large bowl and cover them with boiling water, leave for a minute, drain off, then cover with cold water. The peaches will now peel very easily. Do not do this too early or the fruit will turn brown.

Cut the peaches into halves and remove the stones. Lay the

[31]

halves onto a bed of lettuce hearts and cover with a coating of the dressing. Decorate with a twist of lemon and a couple of sprigs of fresh parsley.

Fresh pears can be substituted if peaches are not available.

Creamed Mushrooms with Croutons

When buying mushrooms choose only those with a pinky-white texture. The brown-looking ones have lost their freshness and flavour.

½ pint milk
½ lb mushrooms
½ oz unsalted butter
½ oz cornflour
2 tablespoons double cream
Salt and black pepper
Squeeze of lemon juice
Fried bread croutons
¼ teaspoon ground nutmeg

Simmer the mushrooms in a little of the milk until soft, about ten minutes. Blend the cornflour to a smooth paste with the remainder of the milk, then add the milk in which the mushrooms were cooked to the cornflour mixture, return this to the pan. Bring to the boil stirring all the time until the mixture thickens, cook for a further three minutes. Stir in the butter and cream, add the salt, pepper and nutmeg, stir in well, then add the lemon juice. Serve hot with the fried bread croutons either as a garnish or served separately.

MEAT DISHES

CRISMIS BEEF

Zom praise vensin, vrim doe or buck,
An zom tha hine laig of a chuck
Zom chicken, goose, turkey, ar duck,
But gie I beef,
That meat'ull put into ee pluck,
An drown yer grief.

Bit spicey beef, ow zweet thy smell,
How zoon thee doost unger dispel,
No other jint can thee excel,
No better voun.
I wish tha butchers ood thee zell
Zixpence a poun.

Zay wat you will, think wat ya med,
I'll stick to it till I be dead,
An ya must vall in we ael I've zed,
Vor 'tis my belief,
There's nothin better for a spread
Than good roast beef.

from *Wiltshire Rhymes* by Edward Slow

[34]

Mr Wadmore's Spiced Hunters Beef

Mr Wadmore was Vicar of Barrow Gurney at about the turn of the century, and gave this recipe to the Gibbs family of Barrow Court. It was always made at Barrow at Christmas time and is now served by Martin Gibbs and his wife at Sheldon Manor near Chippenham, one of Wiltshire's oldest houses. This recipe is one of many good English dishes that are served for lunch in the seventeenth century stables. For today's purposes the weight of beef can naturally be modified to suit your needs, reducing the quantity of ingredients accordingly.

To a round of beef that weighs 25 lbs, take:
4 oz saltpetre
4 oz coarsest brown sugar
1 oz cloves
2 nutmegs
6 bay leaves
½ oz allspice
3 handfuls common salt, all in the finest powder

The beef should hang 2 or 3 days. Then rub the above well into it and turn it and rub in every day for two weeks.

The bone must be taken out first. When to be dressed, dip it into cold water and take off the loose spice. Bind it tight with tape and put it into a large deep pan with 3 inches of water at the bottom. Cover the top of the meat with shredded suet and butter paper (the introduction of aluminium foil has eliminated this process) and tie down over the pan coarse brown paper or lid and bake it 5 or 6 hours according to weight. When done let stand in the liquor until quite cold.

Beef in Wiltshire Beer

A typical dish that might have once been served at the 500 year old Haunch of Venison Inn in Salisbury. Charles Dickens is known to have stayed there on at least one occasion during his visits to the city. It is not unreasonable to assume that it was this inn that gave him the inspiration for Tom Pinch's supper while writing *Martin Chuzzlewit*. Dickens might well have taken such a meal himself.

'... so he (Tom Pinch) had his little table drawn out close before the fire, and fell to work upon a well cooked steak and smoking hot potatoes, with a strong appreciation of their excellence, and a very keen sense of enjoyment. Beside him, too, stood a jug of the most stupendous Wiltshire beer.'

3 lb lean shin of beef
4 oz beef dripping
3 large onions, peeled and chopped
1 clove garlic, crushed with a little salt
Salt and black pepper
2 level tablespoons plain flour
¼ pint beef stock
1 pint Wadsworth's Old Timber beer (or any strong beer)
1 bay leaf
1 sprig of thyme
1 tablespoon dark brown sugar

Melt the dripping in a large pan, cut the beef into ½ inch cubes. Quickly brown the pieces of beef in the hot dripping until golden brown, drain and put into a casserole dish. Lower the heat and cook the onion and crushed garlic together until the onion is a golden brown, put with the beef.

Add the flour and sugar to the pan juices, cook for a few minutes stirring all the time, add the stock a little at a time, stir until smooth. Add the beer, seasonings and bay leaf, pour this into the casserole and cook for 2½ hours at 325°F (160°C), gas mark 3. Serve with hot jacket potatoes topped with butter and a little chopped parsley for garnishing the beef.

Brandied Lamb

The brandy cream sauce turns this traditional joint into a delicious dinner party dish or a rather special Sunday lunch. It is very popular in the restaurant and second helpings are often required. A plump leg of English lamb is ideal for this recipe.

1 large leg lamb
8 tablespoons brandy
8 tablespoons dry white wine
1 oz unsalted butter
1 oz plain flour
2 tins consommé
½ pint double cream
1 tablespoon chopped chives
1 tablespoon caster sugar
Salt and black pepper
Sprig of fresh rosemary

Preheat the oven at 375°F (190°C), gas mark 7.

Place the lamb in a roasting tin with the sprig of rosemary. Add the consommé and white wine, season with the salt and pepper. Place in the centre of the oven and cook for 1½-2 hours. After this time, bring the lamb from the oven and carefully tip off the meat juices into a container, this is for the sauce. Turn the oven heat right down to very low and put the lamb back into the oven.

Skim the fat from the top of the juices. Melt the butter in a saucepan, add the flour and cook for 2 minutes, then add the meat juices, stirring all the time. Should the sauce be to thick, add a little stock or water, or even a little more wine if you wish. Add the chives, sugar and double cream, stir in well. Do not allow the sauce to boil or it will curdle. Keep the sauce warm.

Take the lamb from the oven, heat the brandy in a small saucepan, do not boil. When hot, set alight and pour it over the lamb (this is perfectly safe, for the flame goes out as soon as the brandy makes contact with the lamb). Place the lamb onto a warm serving dish. Add a little water to the roasting tin, stir round and add to the sauce, this is to get all the meat juices and the brandy into the sauce. Slice the lamb and arrange on a hot dish. Pour the sauce over the meat and garnish with sprigs of fresh rosemary and/or fresh parsley. Serve with unskinned, new minted potatoes, the season's first peas, steamed just enough to heat through and tossed with a knob of butter.

Market day in Salisbury in the 1930s.

Cold Meat Mould

In Malmesbury is a lovely Elizabethan country house lying to the north-east of the Abbey from where it takes its name, Abbey House. It was built by William Stumpe, a wealthy clothier, on the monastic foundations. The house is now a rest home for the elderly run by the nuns of the Community of Saint Andrew. This recipe was very kindly given by the cook of Abbey House and is marvellous for using up any left-over meat.

1 lb any cold meat
1 thick slice brown bread
Teacup of stock or a good stock cube
½ small envelope of gelatine
Salt and black pepper

Mince the meat and bread together; season to taste, if the meat is lamb or beef, add a tablespoon of chutney, if pork or chicken, add chopped parsley or other herbs of your choice. Melt the gelatine in the stock and stir into the meat. Pack the mixture into a basin and leave overnight in the larder or refrigerator.

AN OX ROAST AT LANGLEY FITZURSE

An ox was roasted whole in the park, and a troop of yeomanry cavalry guarded it, riding round the ox to keep the people off. When the ox was cut down half of it was burnt and charred and the other half was raw.

While the cavalry were at dinner in the house, the kitchen chimney caught fire. The cavalry rushed out to see what was the matter, and the crowd immediately rushed in and cleared the tables. There was no food to be got in Sutton, all the provisions were swept off.

Kilvert's Diary, December 12th, 1873

To Boil a Ham

If possible, use a Bradenham Ham as it is considered to be the finest of all English-cured ham with its black skin and old fashioned flavour, very different from the pink sweetcure hams of today. Bradenham Ham can be ordered from the Wiltshire Bacon Company in Chippenham, where they have been producing them for nearly one hundred years.

Soak the ham for four days in water to remove the salt, change the liquid a couple of times. After four days, discard the water and put the ham into a large pan and cover with equal quantities of cider and water to which has been added: 1 lb dark brown sugar, 4 large diced carrots, 4 large, peeled and sliced onions, handful black peppercorns, handful pickling spice, 4 sticks chopped celery, 4 bay leaves, and if you have any, a handful of the herb, lovage. Bring slowly to simmering point, skim off any impurities that have risen to the surface. Simmer gently for 3 hours for a 13 lb ham, 3½ hours up to 18 lbs. The liquid must never be allowed to boil, if it does the meat will dry out and become tough. After cooking, leave the ham to cool in the liquid, preferably overnight.

Remove to a dish and cut round the knuckle end to loosen the skin, using a sharp knife strip off the skin. You can if desired leave a collar of black skin and strip off the rest.

Cover with homemade breadcrumbs (10 oz) that have been toasted in the oven at 300°F (150°C), gas mark 2. Put in a cool place for 24 hours. If it is to be stored in the refrigerator between meals wrap it tightly with cling film to prevent drying out. Serve with mustard, pickle or apple mayonnaise (see page   ).

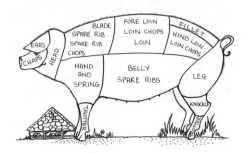

Wiltshire Bacon

As early as the 18th century Wiltshire had a reputation for good bacon. By the 19th century, Wiltshire Bacon meant that it was cured in a particular way. The firm of C&T Harris (Calne) Ltd. played a major roll in maintaining this reputation and in new methods of curing.

John Harris opened a shop at the corner of Calne High Street in 1805-6 and began curing a small quantity of bacon at the back of the shop. Before the construction of the Great Western Railway, large numbers of Irish pigs were driven from Bristol to London and one of the regular stopping places was Calne. These herds became the Harris brothers' main source of supply until 1847 when the shortage of pigs due to the potato famine in Ireland brought the business almost to a standstill. George, younger son of John Harris, left for America to explore the possibility of killing and curing pigs and sending them home to be sold. A shop was opened in New York in 1848 but it was not a success. He returned to England with the knowledge gained from seeing ice-cooled curing houses at work. In 1864, Thomas Harris patented an ice-house after successfully curing bacon in this way in the previous years. With imported ice from Norway and local canal ice they were able to cure bacon throughout the summer.

Early in the 19th century Abraham Bowyer opened a grocery shop in Trowbridge and began to cure bacon almost immediately. When his son, Elijah, took over the store it was described as a wholesale bacon-curers, cheese factor, millers and grocers. The other important activity was the making of sausages.

Most of the other curing companies were small, family firms – few of which survived the 1950s. The Wiltshire Bacon Co. Ltd., incorporated in 1890, provided the Wiltshire farmers with an alternative market for their pigs, the Wiltshire bacon trade having the monopoly. An engineering works was adapted for curing and in 1891 'Royal Wilts' bacon began, making hams, lard, sausages, black puddings, polonies, brawn and cooked Bath chaps. It also took over the Chippenham Cheese factory and, in

1897, took control of the Bradenham Ham Co. Since being wound up in 1921, Bradenham Hams, although still cured by a secret method, have been manufactured by the Wiltshire Bacon Co.

Wiltshire had numerous small curing companies and it would be impossible to list them all. A last tribute to C & T Harris (Calne) Ltd. must be paid, as their foresight, business acumen and expansion gave heart and encouragement to all the other firms in the county. Their permanent closure will be a sad loss not only to Calne but throughout Wiltshire.

Pigs entering C & T Harris's Calne slaughter-house in the 1920s.

To Cure Bacon the Wiltshire Way

This recipe, which is taken from Mrs Beeton's *The Book of Household Management* (1859), is intended to give a short account of how the cottager would have preserved a ham to last throughout the year.

> 1½ lb of coarse sugar
> 1½ lb of bay-salt
> 6 oz saltpetre
> 1 lb common salt

Sprinkle each flitch with salt, and let the blood drain off for 24 hours; then pound and mix the above ingredients well together and rub well into the meat. The flitches should be turned every day for one month; then hung to dry and afterwards to smoke it for 10 days.

Time: to remain in the pickle for one month; to be smoked for 10 days. Sufficient: the above quantity of salt for one pig.

THE GIRT VAT PIG

*I wish that every leabouren man
had a gierden nice and big,
An a leetle stye, kept nice and clane,
An many a girt vat pig.*

*An this I zaays ta wirken voke,
if a meal ya wants a good un,
Cook a ham, an lots a gierden stuff,
An a nice girt figgy pooden.*

Wiltshire Rhymes, Edward Slow

[43]

Wiltshire Ham in Mustard Sauce

Mustard is the essential ingredient in this recipe given by William Tullberg, founder of Wiltshire Tracklement Company at Calne. Their Urchfont Mustard, named after the village near Devizes where it was developed, is made in the old style, by crushing the mustard seeds rather than by grinding as in modern methods.

There is a marvellous range of these mustards which have many subtle and delicious flavours.

1 pint béchamel sauce
2 heaped tablespoons Urchfont Mustard
1 heaped tablespoon grated cheese (Cheddar)
2-3 tablespoons double cream
16 slices thinly cut Wiltshire ham

Make a paste from the mustard, grated cheese, cream, and add to it the béchamel sauce. Arrange the ham slices in an ovenproof dish and pour over the sauce. Top with a little more grated cheese and brown under the grill or in a hot oven.

Wiltshire Gammon in a Cider and Apple Sauce

Cider originally came from Normandy in France and did not spread to the West country until the 13th century. It is made by extracting the juices from apples using a wild yeast for the fermentation and storing it in casks. Gammon cooked in cider has an excellent flavour and with the addition of the apple sauce makes a tasty all the year round lunch dish. In these quantities it serves about 20 and is suitable for a buffet.

10-12 lb ham
2 large carrots, chopped
4 sticks celery, chopped with its leaves
6 cloves
2 large onions, peeled and chopped
Bunch of fresh parsley
1 bay leaf
Water enough to cover the ham

After the ham has been soaked for 4 days (see page 00), put the ham into a large pan with the above ingredients, simmer gently for 3 hours. This can be done the day before it is required and then heated again in the liquid. When required, carefully cut-away the skin from the ham and keep warm while the sauce is being made.

FOR THE SAUCE
2 lb eating apples such as Cox's
2 large onions
1 clove garlic crushed with a little salt
4 sticks celery
4 oz unsalted butter
1 dessert-spoon mustard
½ pint double cream
1 pint sweet cider
1 pint of the liquid that the ham was cooked in
1 tablespoon caster sugar

Peel and core the apples, chop into evenly sized pieces. Peel and slice the onions, chop the celery and crush the garlic with a little salt to form a paste. Melt the butter in a large saucepan, cook the apple, onion, celery and garlic together until the vegetables are soft. Pour in the ham liquid and the cider, simmer for ½ hour uncovered. Taste the sauce before seasoning to prevent over salting.

Liquidize the sauce and lastly add the cream. Serve poured over the thinly sliced gammon.

Cider-making outside the New Inn, Hinton, in November 1939.

Cutlets of Pork with Apple Mayonnaise

Angela's aunt, Iris Syrett, founder of the Tante Marie School of Cookery is responsible for this recipe. It is unusual in that it is served very cold. The apple mayonnaise is well worth the effort, and is very versatile in that it can be used for a variety of dishes or left-over cold meat. Slices of cold pork or chicken are ideal. Being a cold dish it is just right for picnics.

SERVES SIX

6 pork cutlets
3 oz unsalted butter
½ pint mayonnaise (see page 113)
½ lb apple marmalade (see page 118)
2 tablespoons wine based mustard
Fresh herbs, chopped

Trim the cutlets, removing any fat. Melt the butter in a frying pan and cook the cutlets 7-10 minutes on each side according to thickness. Remove from the pan and place on a board, cover with a second board and a heavy weight to flatten them. Allow to get quite cold. Make up the mayonnaise and add the mustard and apple marmalade. Season to taste.

Arrange the cutlets down the centre of a long dish, coat with the mayonnaise mixture and sprinkle with the fresh herbs. Serve with new potatoes and green salad.

Hand-Raised Pork Pie

When we think of pork pies one invariably thinks of Melton Mowbray – the characteristic flavour of Melton Mowbray pork pies is the anchovy essence, which we have included as an optional extra in this recipe. Melton Mowbray may be the traditional home of the pork pie, but the choice of meat makes it also synonymous with Wiltshire.

FOR THE PASTRY
12 oz self-raising flour
½ teaspoon salt
¼ pint water
1 egg (beaten)
4 oz lard

FOR THE FILLING
1¼ lb minced pork
Salt and black pepper
1 sage leaf very finely chopped
1 teaspoon anchovy essence (optional, it does enhance both the colour and flavour though)

FOR THE JELLY
1 lb pork bones or 1 pig's trotter
2 pints water
1 onion
1 teaspoon gelatine
Salt and black pepper

To make the jelly, chop the onion into quarters and put it into a large pan along with the bones or trotter, water and seasoning, simmer for two hours. Strain and add the gelatine which has been previously dissolved in a little cold water over a pan of hot water. Allow to cool but not to set.

To make the hot water crust pastry: sieve the flour and salt into a bowl. Boil the water and lard together in a large pan. Pour this into the centre of the flour and salt while it is still hot. Work well the flour until a smooth dough is formed. Cut off a third of the dough and reserve for the pie lid. The rest is for the pie case.

Using a raised pie mould or warm jam jar the size of your pie, mould the pastry around the outside of the jar or the inside of the mould. This is best done in a warm kitchen as if the pastry is allowed to cool too much it will tend to sink down. If using a jam jar, tie a double band of greaseproof paper around the pastry case before removing the case from the jar. Allow to cool slightly before adding the pork.

Mix all the filling ingredients together and put into the pastry case, put on the lid and seal the edges with the beaten egg. Decorate if wished with pastry leaves or roses. Brush again with the egg and make a hole in the centre of the lid.

Bake at 400°F (200°C), gas mark 6 for 30 minutes then reduce the heat to 358°F (180°C), gas mark 4 for 1¾ hours.

Allow the pie to cool after cooking and pour the jelly mixture through the hole which you have made in the lid.

Completely chill before serving. A green salad, a fresh tomato and basil salad, accompanied by home-made chutneys will go very well with this pie.

Burning the hairs off a cottager's pig before curing and smoking, near Trowbridge in the early 1900s.

Pork Tenderloin with a Brandy, Apple and Cream Sauce

This recipe uses the fillet, the best cut of pork. Though expensive, there are no bones and no waste and when flattened into an escallop it is a very quick dish to make. Ideal for a dinner party when accompanied by the brandy and apple sauce.

SIX SERVINGS

3 large pork tenderloins
3 oz unsalted butter
4 tablespoons vegetable oil
Sherry glass of brandy
4 dessert-spoons apple marmalade (see page 118)
¼ pint chicken stock
3 good flavoured eating apples
Juice of 1 large lemon
½ pint double cream
Salt and black pepper

Remove the fat and any sinew from the pork and cut into 2 inch cubes. Wet the surface of a piece of marble or formica table top; place a piece of pork onto the marble or table top, cover with a piece of cling film dampened on the side next to the meat. Take a rolling pin and firmly flatten the pork to form an escallop. Repeat this process until all the pork pieces are used up. Wetting the pork and working surface prevents the meat from sticking.

Melt the butter and oil in a large pan, this should be fairly hot, but take care not to burn the butter. Sauté the pork escallops quickly on both sides, do not over cook, the heat only needs to get through the meat to seal in the juices. After all the pork has been sautéd, cover and keep warm.

Peel and chop the apple into chunks and sauté in the pan until golden brown. Keep warm until required. Pour the brandy into the pan, let the bubbles subside then set alight the brandy. Make sure that you have plenty of space above the pan and do not stand too close. When the flames have subsided, add the stock, lemon juice, apple marmalade, apple pieces and the seasonings. Simmer until reduced by half.

Finally, pour the cream into the pan, stirring all the time, blend in all the ingredients well. Check the seasoning. Pour the sauce over the pork and serve sprinkled with chopped, fresh parsley, new potatoes, and a tossed green salad.

A Wiltshire labourer enjoying his 'nammet', or lunch,
near Teffont in about 1895.

Pork Chops with Juniper Berries and Gin

The oil-rich crushed berries of the prickly evergreen shrub Juniper are the principal ingredient for flavouring gin. During their first year, they have a similarity to small green cones, and it is not until their second year, when they turn black, that they are ready for picking. The juniper is not so widespread on the Downs as it used to be, indeed many have been choked by elder and hawthorn due to the decline in the rabbit population. Juniper berries are an excellent flavouring for veal as well as pork, and the dried berries are obtainable from good supermarkets.

8 pork chops
16 juniper-berries, crushed
Small wine glass of gin
¼ pint white stock, chicken or veal
¼ pint double cream
2 dessert-spoons redcurrant jelly
Lemon juice to taste
Salt and black pepper
Oil for cooking

Marinade the pork chops in the gin and crushed juniper berries, season well, cover, and leave for at least 4 hours or overnight.

Drain the chops and dry off with kitchen paper, reserve the marinade for the sauce. Fry the chops in the oil for 10-15 minutes on each side, keep warm on a large dish. Deglaze the frying pan by pouring in the marinade and the stock, stir firmly to remove the meat juices that may be still on the bottom of the pan, add the redcurrant jelly, and season again, cook until the jelly has melted and the liquid reduced to a syrupy sauce. Finally add the cream. Add a little lemon juice if you would prefer a sharper tasting sauce.

Serve with broad beans, baby carrots cooked in a little orange juice, and new potatoes (with skins).

Loin of Pork with a Lemon and Mushroom Sauce

We often cook this dish during late summer and autumn when field mushrooms are to be found growing on the gallops in the dense pasture of the Marlborough Downs just 10 minutes from Rockley. A damp, misty morning finds us suitably booted against the saturating dew up on the Downs with a large wicker basket intently quartering the grass in the hope of finding the creamy white caps of the field mushroom. There was a time when fields would experience a 'white-out' – when the right temperature, soil condtion and humidity would produce so many mushrooms that the field seemed to be covered with snow. We can, of course, buy cultivated mushrooms and for this recipe they are an adequate substitute, but for taste and sheer satisfaction, there is – for us – nothing quite like finding and cooking 'wild' field mushrooms.

4 lb loin of pork, boned and rolled

FOR THE SAUCE
6 oz unsalted butter
10 oz field or button mushrooms, thinly sliced
3 oz plain flour
1½ pints milk
2 teaspoons freshly chopped herbs
(any combination of parsley, chives, thyme etc.)
Juice and finely grated rind of 2 lemons
1 dessert-spoon caster sugar
Salt and black pepper
Chopped fresh parsley to garnish

Roast the pork at 400°C (200°C), gas mark 6 for ¾ hour, then reduce the heat to 375°F (190°C), gas mark 5 and cook for a further 1¼ hours. Put 3 oz of the butter into a saucepan, add the mushrooms and cook over a gentle heat until they change colour, stir all the time. Remove the mushrooms and put to one side until required for the sauce. Put the remaining butter into another saucepan, when it has melted add the flour, cook for 2 minutes then add the milk a little at a time, beat it well. You may not require all the milk as the texture must not be too runny. Add the herbs, lemon juice, rind, sugar, mushrooms and the melted butter, season well.

When the meat is ready, skim off any fat from the meat juices that are left in the pan and tip the remaining juice into the sauce, blend in well.

Slice the meat thinly and arrange on a hot serving dish, pour the sauce over the meat, garnish with the chopped parsley and serve with braised parsnips, buttered carrots and creamed potatoes.

A farmer on the Marlborough Downs appears to have paid the phenomenal amount of 18s. per week during harvest, his reapers sometimes earning 10s. per day, enough to pay their years rent in a week. These men also received from 6-8 quarts of beer per man every day during this period, and many farmers paid £50 or £60 a year on this cheering beverage in order to see that all was 'safely gathered in'.

Portrait of Wiltshire, Pamela Street

Market Day Casserole

John Aubrey in his *Natural History of Wiltshire* mentions a few of the better Wiltshire markets that he visited in the 17th century. Warminster, thought to be the greatest market for corn and coach horses, was held on Saturdays. Devizes, famed for fish which came up from Poole, was on Thursdays, though there must have been one other market day as there is a Monday Market Street in the centre of the town. Marlborough, held on Saturdays, was renowed for being the greatest cheese market in the West. Castle Coombe sold eggs, butter and cheese on Mondays. Hindon was second only to Warminster for wheat.

Inns too played an important part on market day, being a general meeting place and providing banking and storage facilities as well as food and drink. Dishes similar to this casserole would be served as part of the 'Farmers Ordinary', a meal taken at the conclusion of the day's business. Alternatively, it would have been kept on the fire waiting for the family to return home after selling their produce.

8 pork chops
3 apples, peeled, cored and sliced
1 lb onions, peeled and sliced
1½ lb potatoes, peeled and sliced
1 teaspoon chopped sage
1 teacup cider or stock
1 teacup water
Salt and black pepper

Pre-heat the oven to 240°F (120°C), gas mark ½.

Place a layer of sliced potato and onion on the bottom of a casserole dish; choose a fairly deep dish to accommodate all the ingredients. Add a little salt and pepper, then a couple of pork chops, next a layer of apple and sage. Repeat the layers reserving sufficient potato to cover the top of the casserole. Pour the cider or stock over the ingredients, add the teacup of water and season again. Cover the dish with a lid or tin foil and cook for 2½ hours until the meat is tender. Test the meat by putting a fork into the chops, if the fork comes out easily then it is ready, if it still feels slightly tough, cook a little longer.

Take the lid off the casserole for the last ½ hour of cooking to allow the potatoes to brown.

BEEANS AN BEAKIN

I tell ee what it is me bwoys,
You mid praise beef, and mutton,
An geam, an pawltry, an zish like
Ta I, teant woth a button.

Now var a veed jist let I have,
An dwoant ee be misteaken,
Tha vinest veast in ael the wordle,
Is one, a beeans an beakin.

When you'm at work apon the varm
A mawin, ar haymeakin,
Ther's nuthen that ull stan be ee,
Like a veed a beeans an beakin.

Hache Zunday, when thame nice and vit,
We veeds, on beeans an beakin,
An a nice girt apple crowdy too,
Main good me wife da meakin.

Voke zaays I'll zoon get tired on't,
Mid my yead never be yeakin*
Till I da gie up, gettin outzide
A platter a beeans an beakin.

*Mid (may), Yead (head), Yeakin (aching)

Wiltshire Rhymes, Edward Slow

[56]

Mutton or Lamb Patties

Until the 18th century sheep were bred for their wool, and it was only the weaker animals from the flock that were eaten. Mutton was usually about four years old when eaten, and was roasted in the same way as the draught oxen, which was often the only meat the poor ever ate. It was extremely tough and required long hours of stewing. Being much more tender than ox, mutton soon became highly favoured. These days mutton is quite difficult to come by. It is cheaper than lamb, and although not as tender it has more flavour. If you cannot buy mutton, a large, lean leg of lamb will suffice.

2 lb minced mutton or lamb
1 large onion, peeled and minced
1 teaspoon chopped parsley
½ teaspoon chopped tarragon or thyme
Salt and black pepper
½ teaspoon ground nutmeg
1 small clove garlic, crushed with a little salt (optional)
4 oz brown breadcrumbs
3 eggs, beaten

Combine all the ingredients together thoroughly, and form into round, flat cakes. Chill them well in the refrigerator.

When required, fry in hot fat for 7 minutes on each side until golden brown. Serve with caper sauce (see page 00) braised parsnips and boiled, parsley potatoes.

Mutton Pie

During the Victorian era, mutton was almost the inevitable joint served at dinner parties, particulary by the middle classes. Sadly, mutton today has gone out of fashion, but if you can get hold of this splendid meat you will not be disappointed, though of course lamb can be substituted.

2 lb neck or loin of mutton or lamb
2 kidneys
2 teacupfuls of gravy or stock
2 tablespoons chopped parsley
1 small onion, chopped
Puff pastry for the crust
Salt and pepper to taste

Bone the meat and cut into small pieces; cut the kidney and put these along with the meat into a pie dish; sprinkle over the chopped parsley and add the seasoning. Pour in the gravy or stock and add the chopped onion. Cover with the rolled puff pastry and brush with beaten egg.

Bake in a preheated oven 400°F (200°C), gas mark 8, for the first 25 minutes, then lower the temperature to 300°F (150°C), gas mark 5 for a further 1½ hours. The pastry should turn a lovely golden brown colour. It will be necessary to cover the pastry when it reaches the golden brown stage to prevent burning while the meat is cooking. Greaseproof paper placed over the crust will stop the pastry from cooking further.

A suet crust will be found to be rather good as an alternative to puff pastry. Serve with fresh green vegetables and creamed potatoes.

Country Fry

After the autumn killing of the cottage pig there was a surplus of offal which in the days before refrigerators and freezers could not be preserved. The wealthier yeomen farmers would add chops and bacon to such things as brains, liver and kidney in a large black skillet over the fire. With the few extras that we have added a simple meal is turned into a feast.

TO SERVE FOUR

2 oz unsalted butter
2 tablespoons chopped parsley
2 leaves sage
4 medium onions, peeled and sliced
4 rashers bacon
4 pork chops
8 oz pigs liver cut into 4 thin slices
2 pigs kidneys skinned, cores removed and sliced
1 oz seasoned flour
4 tomatoes blanched, skinned and cut in half
8 oz mushrooms, cleaned and sliced
2 slices white bread cut into small squares

Heat two large frying pans, put the butter into one and the bacon into the other. Fry the onion gently in the butter. When the bacon is crisp, remove from the pan, put onto a large serving dish and keep warm.

Dip the liver, chops and kidneys into the flour and fry them in the bacon pan, until cooked through. Turn the meat so that it browns on both sides. Turn the onions from time to time, then push to one side of the pan and add the tomatoes and mushrooms. When all is cooked put with the bacon and arrange on the serving dish, again keep warm. Pour into the bacon pan any fat that is left from the offal pan and fry the bread cubes until golden brown. Arrange these around the serving dish and sprinkle over the chopped herbs. Serve at once. Sauté potatoes can also be added if you are really hungry.

Home-made Sausages

Sausage skins are not that easy to find, but a good butcher can order them for you. However, these sausages can be made skinless. Just roll the mixture into shape, cut to the required length, dust with flour and lightly fry. Our butcher, Mr Mills of Ramsbury, gave us this recipe but we have adapted the quantity of the ingredients on the assumption that you would not wish to make a hundred sausages at a time.

TO MAKE 15-20 SAUSAGES DEPENDING ON LENGTH

2 lb very lean pork, finely minced
8 oz fresh white breadcrumbs
¼ teaspoon grated nutmeg
1½ teaspoons salt
½ teaspoon freshly ground black pepper
½ teaspoon powdered marjoram
½ teaspoon powdered thyme
½ teaspoon powdered sage
12 oz shredded suet

Put all the ingredients into a large bowl and mix them thoroughly, making sure that the herbs and seasonings are well distributed.

Should you have skins, put the mixture into a forcing bag with a wide nozzle, knot one end of skin, choose your required length and cut away from the rest of the skin. Push the bag into the length of skin until it touches the knot and force the meat into the skin. Do not over fill. Knot the other end and repeat until all the meat and/or skin is used up. Allow the sausages to rest before cooking or storing.

The suggested herbs and seasonings are just a guide, you can have fun creating your own sausages by using whatever flavourings you prefer.

Labourers enjoying a mid-day break near All Cannings in the late 1920s.

THE WILTSHIRE LABOURER

'the lumbering gait of the Wiltshire labourer around Swindon was the result of walking behind the plough in early childhood, when weak limbs found it hard labour to pull heavy nailed boots from the thick clay soil; furthermore, their diet had something to do with this seeming lack of vitality, as it consisted of bread and cheese, soft oil bacon twice or thrice a week (occasionally enhanced by onions) while, if a man happened to be a milker, he enjoyed a good tuck in at his employers expense on Sundays.'

Letter to *The Times*. November 1872, *Richard Jefferies*

Ramsbury Faggots

Faggots were a popular way of using up any scraps left over from the killing of the pig. They would include the liver, melts, and heart. Some butchers use belly of pork, as in this second recipe given to us by Gilbert Mills of Ramsbury. His is a small family business first started by his grandfather, Alfred Mills, in 1900 at Hungerford, who bought his first shop for ten, half gold sovereigns.

These faggots are made on the premises, as they have been since Gilbert's father started the Ramsbury business in 1938.

2 lb belly of pork
3 large eggs, beaten
2 lb streaky bacon
1 pig's heart
½ lb pig's liver
1½ lb brown breadcrumbs
1 onion, peeled and chopped
Nutmeg, ginger, sage, pepper, thyme, salt, all to taste
Piece of caul fat, about 1 lb (your butcher should sell this)

Chop the pork, bacon, liver and heart. Add the seasonings and the onion, then pass through a mincer. Put the minced mixture into a large bowl, add the breadcrumbs and bind together with the beaten egg. Form into small balls. Soften the caul fat in a bowl of luke warm water. Cut into squares, sufficient in size to wrap round the faggots. Place the wrapped faggots onto a baking tray, pour a little stock over each faggot to prevent them from drying out, bake in the oven 400°F (200°C), gas mark 5 for a good hour.

Wiltshire Meat Paste

This paste would have graced many a tea table in the larger country houses, and undoubtedly been taken on a picnic. It is delicious when spread on hot toast or thinly sliced buttered bread. This very simple recipe is taken from *Wiltshire Miscellany* by J.A. Leete.

1 lb lean beef
1 tablespoon anchovy paste or essence
½ teaspoon ground black pepper
Salt to taste
½ grated nutmeg

Put all the ingredients into a large basin after mincing thoroughly. Steam for at least 2 hours. Allow to cool before spreading.

To Make Lard

Melt the inner fat of the pig, by putting it in a stone jar, and placing this in a saucepan of boiling water, previously stripping off the skin. Let it simmer gently over a bright fire, and as it melts, pour it carefully from the sediment. Put it into small jars or bladders for use, and keep it in a cool place. The flead or inside fat of the pig, before it is melted, makes exceedingly light crust, and is particularly wholesome. It may be preserved a length of time by salting it well, and occasionally changing the brine. When wanted for use, wash and wipe it, and it will answer for making into paste as well as fresh lard.

Average cost 10d per pound.

from *The Book of Household Management* (1959)

Oxtail Stew

Oxtails are usually sold ready to cook. One tail serves three to four. They were much relished by the country poor. The term oxtail has survived even though now applied to beef cattle.

2 whole jointed oxtails
4 carrots, peeled and sliced
2 onions, peeled and sliced
1 clove garlic, crushed with a little salt
1 turnip, peeled and sliced
1 oz beef dripping
1 oz plain flour
4 rashers streaky bacon
½ pint beef stock
¼ pint red wine
1 bay leaf
Large sprig fresh parsley
1 small leek (not to be included in the browning of the vegetables)
Large sprig fresh thyme
Salt and black pepper

Take the vegetables and brown them in the beef dripping, add the garlic to the pan and stir into the vegetables. Put the vegetables into a casserole dish.

Toss the jointed oxtails in the flour, brown in the remaining dripping, put the pieces into the casserole.

Cut the leek in half lengthways, place the herbs in the centre and tie together with string, put into the casserole.

Chop the bacon and add to the casserole, pour over the stock and wine, season, cover and cook for 3 hours at 325°F (170°C), gas mark 3. After this time, the meat should be tender. Remove any fat from the surface, check the seasoning and sprinkle with chopped parsley. Serve with herb dumplings, buttered cabbage, boiled potatoes and home-made bread.

POULTRY AND GAME

Hawking, netting and snaring game were common practice on the Downs and Salisbury Plain until the Enclosure Acts of the late-18th and early 19th-centuries and the increased ploughing that followed. Thrushes, fieldfares, partridges, rabbits and the great bustard were all considered good sport by gentlemen and working men alike.

The great bustard was traditionally eaten at the Mayor of Salisbury's inaugural feast and appears on Wiltshire's coat of arms. Its size, the appeal of its eggs, and the gradual loss of its breeding territory on the Plain, led to its extinction in about 1820. In recent years, The Great Bustard Trust has reintroduced the bustard into Britain and a small group of the birds have been released onto Porton Down in the hope that they will successfully breed.

Hare coursing with greyhounds was possibly the widest practised sport in the county until fox-hunting became popular towards the end of the 18th century. The open Plain provided the perfect habitat for hares and the decline of coursing was partially due to the Ground Game Act of 1880, which gave tenant farmers equal rights with their landlords to the hares and rabbits on their land.

Netting was another popular way of catching game for the table. Partridges were caught in this manner. A pointer, or setting dog, held the birds to ground whilst a net, held by two men, was carefully drawn over the birds. Sometimes a dog would be used to gradually work the covey into the net. Duck were also netted at the edge of ponds where they flighted. Tame birds were tied and pinioned and used as decoys to lure the wild birds into a long tapering net, and dogs were used to work the duck into the narrowed neck of the net.

Hawking was once common on the Plain and Downs. Sir Ralph Sadler, falconer to Elizabeth I, held the manor at Everleigh and trained and flew falcons from there. Hawking on the Plain has now almost died out. The Old Hawking Club had its headquarters at the Bustard Inn, Shrewton, in the late-19th century but the Club was dissolved in the mid-1920s. Rook were hawked during March and April, whilst peregrines and merlins were used for taking partridges and larks during August.

Chicken Suet Pudding with Prunes

A deliciously different dish for a winter's Sunday lunch, a homely, and attractive main course when served upon a board or dish with a white napkin wrapped around the pudding basin.

1 lb self-raising flour
8 oz suet
1 chicken
1 onion, chopped
1 bay leaf
¼ pint chicken stock
8 oz prunes, soaked overnight and stones removed

Mix the flour and suet together, form into a firm dough with cold water. Line a 2 pint pudding basin with ⅓ of the dough, reserving the remainder for the top of the pudding. Cut the meat from the breast and legs of the chicken, put the carcass with the giblets into a saucepan, add the juice from the soaked prunes, simmer gently for 1½ hours then strain through a sieve. This is for the gravy.

Toss the chicken pieces in a little seasoned flour. Fill the lined basin with alternate layers of chicken, prunes, and onion, seasoning as you go. Put the bay leaf in the centre of the pudding. Pour in the chicken stock, cover with the remaining suet pastry, then seal with a double layer of foil. Steam for 4 hours. Serve with the gravy poured over buttered creamed potatoes and nutmeg seasoned carrots.

Roast Goose with Spiced Pickled Pears

There is an old country saying that if you eat goose on Michaelmas Day (September 29th) you will never want for money all the year. Unfortunately, we have not yet had this proved to us, nevertheless we shall continue to eat goose at Michaelmas, especially when accompanied by the spiced pears.

1 goose, plucked and cleaned ready for the oven
6 oz minced pork
4 oz minced veal
1 onion, finely chopped
1 clove garlic, crushed with a little salt
1 oz unsalted butter
4 oz wholemeal breadcrumbs
4 oz hazelnuts, roughly chopped
1 egg beaten with a little milk
1 tablespoon parsley, chopped
¼ pint sweet white wine
a little milk for binding the stuffing
4 sticks celery, chopped

Fry the onion and celery in the unsalted butter until they are soft, add the garlic. Remove from the heat and add all the rest of the ingredients except the wine and bind together with the egg and milk. Season to taste.

Put the stuffing inside the goose and cook in a very hot oven 450°F (240°C), gas mark 8 for 30 minutes, then lower the temperature to 350°F (180°C), gas mark 4. Allow 15 minutes to the pound. Baste frequently with the wine during cooking. When cooked, remove from the oven and put onto a hot dish.

Take 6 of the spiced pears (see below for spiced pears) and chop roughly, remove core and stalks. Remove as much fat as possible from the goose juices and add the chopped pears along with a little spiced pear syrup. Stir well and add a little hot water to blend the juices.

Liquidize the sauce or if preferred leave it with the pear pieces. Arrange a few whole spiced pears around the dish and serve with the sauce poured over the goose or separately in a sauce boat.

SPICED PICKLED PEARS

6 lb good firm pears
3 lb granulated sugar
½ pint white wine vinegar
1 cinnamon stick
1 tablespoon crushed black peppercorns
1 tablespoon cloves
1 bay leaf

Peel the pears leaving them whole and with their stalks intact. Place them in a large bowl and cover with cold salted water.

In a saucepan dissolve the sugar in the wine vinegar, add the spices tied in a piece of muslin. Take the pears out of the salted water and put them into the spiced liquid. Simmer gently until the pears are soft, but not too soft or they will spoil. When cooked, put the pears into warm, clean preserving jars along with the spiced syrup that they have been cooked in, cover firmly. Label and store until required.

Spiced pears would go equally well with roast pork as a change from apple sauce.

Casserole of Rabbit in Elderberry Wine

Rabbit improves with marinading, preferably overnight. White wine or lemon juice in the marinade can be used unless other ingredients are to be used as is the case in this recipe.

1 rabbit

FOR THE MARINADE
¼ pint elderberry wine (see page 121)
3 tablespoons vegetable oil
1 clove garlic crushed with a little salt
1 large onion, peeled and sliced
6 crushed juniper berries
Black pepper
1 bay leaf
1 sprig of thyme

Mix the above ingredients in a large bowl, joint the rabbit and place the pieces into the marinade. Leave for 24 hours or overnight. Turn the rabbit occasionally.

REMAINDER OF INGREDIENTS
4 oz rindless smoked bacon, chopped
2 oz unsalted butter
1 tablespoon vegetable oil
2 onions, chopped
1 pint elderberry wine
½ pint chicken stock
1 heaped tablespoon cornflour
2 teaspoons mustard

Melt the butter and oil together in a large frying pan; add the chopped bacon and fry until just crisp, remove from the pan and put into a casserole. Fry the onions in the fat until golden brown then add to the casserole also.

Dry the rabbit pieces and fry until golden brown; add to the casserole. Pour the marinade juices into the frying pan and

[70]

simmer until it reaches the consistency of syrup. Add the chicken stock to the marinade along with the elderberry wine. Strain the liquid over the rabbit, add the mustard and season to taste. Cover and cook for 1½-2 hours until tender.

After the cooking time is up, remove the pieces of rabbit and keep warm; skim off any fat from the juices, add the cornflour slackened with a little water and thicken the liquid. Check the seasoning.

Put the rabbit back into the casserole and serve with fried bread croutons, creamed potatoes and red cabbage cooked with apple and onion.

Rabbit Pie

Mary Roberts, who has lived in the country all her life, gave us this recipe. She assures us that if the rabbit for the pie has been feeding on the sweet herb-strewn turf of the Wiltshire Downs, so much the better. We have eaten many meals in her herring-bone tiled cottage nestling by Rockley village pond, and her rabbit pie has always been one of our favourites.

1 skinned and jointed rabbit (see page 75)
2 oz lard
1 slice ham or bacon
2 shelled hard boiled eggs, sliced
¼ lb mushrooms
2 tablespoons plain flour
¼ teaspoon salt
¼ teaspoon nutmeg
Shake of pepper
Pinch of pepper
Pinch of mace
Good stock
Shortcrust pastry

FOR THE GRAVY

Rabbit bones
Small onion
Fresh herbs
Cornflour for thickening
Wine glass of sherry
Wine glass of water

To make the gravy: chop the onion and put into a saucepan along with the rabbit bones, wine, water and herbs. Simmer for ½ hour. Strain the gravy into a basin, discarding the bones. Put the gravy back into the pan with the cornflour, cook, stirring all the time until it thickens. Season to taste, put to one side until required.

After having boned the rabbit, roll the meat in a little seasoned flour, (i.e. salt, pepper, mace, nutmeg).

Fry lightly in a little lard, place the rabbit in a pie dish, and add the mushrooms. Add the sliced egg and the ham or bacon. Pour over a little stock, cover with shortcrust pastry, bake in a moderate oven for about 2 hours. Should the pastry brown too quickly, cover with greaseproof paper. The long cooking time is to ensure that the rabbit meat is really tender. Serve straight from the oven with the hot, thick gravy and a purée of creamed parsnips with nutmeg and sautéed potato cakes cooked in bacon fat.

A Swindon butcher's shop in 1887.

Farley's Jugged Hare

Farley was a carter in the hamlet of Rockley at the turn of the century. He lived in a whitewashed Tudor cottage by the pond, whose thatched roof reaching almost down to the ground at the back of the house resembles a cottage loaf. The sale of Rockley Manor and farm meant that Farley, along with the blacksmith, the school mistress, and the farm labourers had to leave the hamlet for employment elsewhere, but Farley's cottage still retains his name today. It is now occupied by Mrs Joan Stevens, herself a retired school mistress. This dish is cooked regularly at Farley's, and was named in the old carter's honour.

1 hare, jointed
Beef stock enough to cover the meat
2 medium sized onions, peeled and sliced
Juice of ½ lemon
Salt and black pepper
A few cloves
Oil and butter, equal quantities to fry the hare
Tablespoon redcurrant jelly
Large glass red wine

Fry the joints of hare in the butter and oil to seal in the juices; place them in a casserole dish with the beef stock. Add the onion, lemon juice cloves and the seasonings. Cook in the oven until the meat is tender, 325°F (170°C), gas mark 3. When cooked, allow to cool.

Once cool, discard the cloves, remove the flesh from the bones and return the meat to the casserole dish. Add the redcurrant jelly and the red wine. Reheat the casserole; adjust the seasoning and thicken the gravy by removing the meat and boiling until the liquid is reduced by half. Serve with a large chunk of homemade, wholemeal bread, a purée of carrot and parsnip, and well-seasoned creamed potatoes to soak up the juices.

To Skin and Joint a Hare or Rabbit

Hare is available in the shops between August and February.

Rabbit, which is now specially bred for the table is usually eaten when 3-3½ months old. Fresh or frozen rabbits are normally bought ready prepared, skinned, paunched and jointed. They can be prepared at home in the same way as a hare, except they are not hung like the hare.

Hare is usually sold already hung. If it is not, it should be hung by its feet for 7-10 days. Place a bowl under the head to collect the blood, which can be used to thicken the gravy. A few drops of vinegar added to the bowl prevents the blood from coagulating.

To skin; lay the hare or rabbit on several sheets of paper and cut off the feet using a sharp knife. Slit the skin along the belly and ease it away from the flesh. Pull the skin over the hind legs, then pull it towards the head, ease the skin over the forelegs and over the head.

Paunching (removing the entrails); slit the belly from the hind legs towards the head. Draw out the internal organs, reserving the kidneys, heart and liver for making gravy or sauce. Mind you do not break the gall bladder as it will impart a bitter taste. Discard all other organs. Catch the blood in a basin for gravy.

Jointing; cut the skinned and cleaned animal into eight joints. Using a sharp knife, cut off the skin flaps below the rib cage and discard. Divide the carcase in half lengthways along the backbone, cut off the hind legs at the top of the thigh, breaking the bone. Cut off the forelegs around the shoulder. Cut each half in two.

The section between the forelegs and hind legs is known as the 'saddle' and if this is to be roasted whole, cut off the belly flaps, forelegs and hind legs as described. If a hare, do not slit through the backbone.

Steak and Pigeon Pie

Pigeons are one of the easiest birds to pluck. There is no close season for pigeons but they are at their plumpest between May and October, when they have been feeding on the ripening wheat and barley. You can buy ready-prepared pigeons from any of the better supermarkets and though not as full of flavour they are excellent when added to steak as in this recipe.

8 oz puff pastry
1 egg, beaten for the glaze
4 pigeons, cut in half
1 onion, chopped
2 oz unsalted butter
1 lb stewing beef
4 rashers streaky bacon
½ pint strong chicken stock
¼ lb mushrooms, sliced
½ tablespoon made mustard
Salt and black pepper
1 tablespoon redcurrant jelly
1 tablespoon plain flour
A little lemon juice

Fry the pigeon halves until brown to seal in the juices, put them into a large casserole dish. Cut the steak into cubes and fry these also until brown, add to the pigeons. Fry the bacon until the fat begins to run, add to the casserole. Brown the onion in the bacon fat, stir in the flour and cook for about 1 minute, pour in the stock and stir. Add the mushrooms, mustard, lemon juice redcurrant jelly and the seasonings. Stir well together, pour this liquid over the meat.

Cover and cook in a moderate oven for at least 2 hours until the pigeon meat falls away from the bone. Allow to cool, then remove the pigeon bones. Put the meat into a pie dish and place a pie funnel in the centre. Cover with the pastry and brush with beaten egg. Put into a very hot oven to cook the pastry then lower the heat so as to heat up the meat for about ¾ hour. Serve with creamed potatoes and fresh green vegetables.

Potted Pheasant with Crab Apple Jelly

Potted meats or game are usually seasoned and cooked until tender, then pounded to a paste, potted and covered with melted butter. Alternatively, they can be left whole in the cooking pot and then covered with the melted butter.

Potted meats, or indeed fish, are a good way of making a good dish from cooked or uncooked leftovers. They can be stored in a cool place such as a refrigerator, or larder for up to 2 months in winter. Once the butter seal is broken, they must be eaten within 2 days.

To clarify butter put it into a pan and allow it to melt, carefully skim off the butterfat and pour over the potted meat, discard the whey which is underneath the fat.

2 lb cooked minced pheasant
½ pint rich jellied game stock
1 sherry glass of cream sherry or port
1 teaspoon ground nutmeg
½ clove garlic crushed with a little salt
Clarified butter
4 fresh bay leaves
Salt and ground black pepper

Put the minced pheasant into a bowl, melt the stock then add the port or sherry. Pour this onto the pheasant and mix well together; add the seasonings. Add the crushed garlic and the nutmeg to the pheasant mixture and beat well. Press the mixture into a large paté dish or individual ramekins, top with the clarified butter and decorate with the bay leaves.

Serve as a light lunch dish with salad or as a first course with the crab apple jelly and hot bread.

(For crab apple jelly see page 119).

Pheasant Casserole with Chestnuts

Most good butchers have a plentiful supply of pheasant during the game season, and for a nominal charge will normally pluck and draw them for you. Supermarkets too are getting in a tentative supply of oven ready pheasant so you should have no difficulty in obtaining a brace or two. Of course you may be lucky enough to live near an estate that would sell you a small number of pheasant direct.

Ripe chestnuts begin to fall in late October but the best time to pick them is in mid-November. The spiny husks will have dropped away leaving the nuts lying among the leaves and the whole task is less painful.

To prepare fresh chestnuts; make a hole in each nut and place in a saucepan. Cover with cold water and simmer for ½ hour. Remove the skins using a sharp knife. This takes a little time but is well worth the effort. If you do not have the time to gather the chestnuts, or do not have a supply near you, tinned chestnuts can be used but they must be natural and not the sweetened variety. Fresh chestnuts are available in most greengrocers as Christmas approaches.

Brace of pheasant
3 lb chestnuts or 2 tins whole, natural chestnuts
1 lb button mushrooms
½ lb streaky bacon, chopped
2 bay leaves
2 tablespoons plain flour
1 tablespoon parsley, chopped
Dripping to brown the pheasant
1 tin consommé
3 tablespoons redcurrant jelly or plum jam
¼ bottle dry white wine
1 glass port
1 oz unsalted butter
½ pint beef stock
Salt and black pepper

Preheat the oven to 350°F (175°C), gas mark 4.

Dry the pheasant and dust with a little flour. Fry the bacon and the onion, cook until soft, remove from the pan and put to one side. Add a little more dripping to the pan and fry the pheasants one at a time until brown all over. Place the fried pheasant into a casserole.

Melt the 1 oz butter in the pan and add enough flour to absorb the fat. Add the tin of consommé, stock, port, wine, redcurrant jelly or plum jam, mix well together, add salt and pepper to taste. Put the mushrooms with the pheasant along with the fried bacon and onions, pour over the sauce and cook for 2½ hours until the pheasant is tender.

When the pheasant is cooked, divide it into portions for serving, it is easier to do this when cooked as it is more difficult when raw. Any good kitchen shop or hardware store should sell poultry scissors if you do not already have any; they are stronger and easier to use for this job than ordinary kitchen scissors.

While the pheasant is cooking prepare the chestnuts then add them to the sauce just before serving. Serve with creamed potatoes and brussels sprouts.

Roast Partridge with Celeriac Purée

In the 17th and 18th centuries partridges were of the greatest, economic importance owing to their immense numbers and the ease in which they were taken. Edie, in his *Treatise on English Shooting* (1773) remarks: 'Partridge shooting, on account of the cleanness, little fatigue, and more certain diversion than any other, by their being found in coveys, and taking short flights, is generally esteemed the genteelest and best sport we have in England.'

Even today, many people consider the partridge to be their favourite game bird. A young bird shot in September needs only to be hung 3-5 days. An older bird will need about 10 days hanging but watch for any discolouration.

2 partridge plucked and drawn
2 large knobs of butter
2 strips of pork fat or streaky bacon
salt and black pepper

FOR THE PUREE

1 large celeriac, peeled and chopped into small cubes
1 onion, peeled and chopped
½ pint chicken stock
2 oz butter
salt and black pepper
4 oz single cream

Lay the birds breast side down in a roasting tin. Put a knob of butter inside each bird, season well then lay the pork fat or bacon over the birds. Roast for 30 minutes 425°F (220°C), gas mark 7, then lower the temperature to 400°F (200°C), gas mark 6, turn the birds breast side up and brown for a further 10-15 minutes.

To make the purée; melt the butter in a large suacepan and add the chopped celeriac and onion, cook until soft, then add

[80]

the chicken stock and simmer gently for 20 minutes. Season to taste and add the cream, liquidize to a smooth paste.

Serve the partidges decorated with celery leaves if you have them or sprigs of fresh parsley, golden roast potatoes, brussels sprouts and the celeriac purée.

Wiltshire fare. October 1939 near Alton Priors in the Vale of Pewsey.

Wild Duck with a Port and Blackberry Sauce

Though we have suggested using wild duck, the farmyard or Aylesbury duck can be substituted with equal success as the main theme of this recipe is the sauce. The sweetness of the fruit compliments the richness of the duck, especially wild duck. If the blackberries are juicy and sweet a little more lemon juice can be added.

2 ducks
2 oz unsalted butter
½ pint port wine
1 lb blackberries
¼ pint fresh orange juice
1 tablespoon caster sugar
6 rashers smokey bacon
Juice of ½ lemon
Salt and black pepper

Pre-set the oven to 350°F (180°C), gas mark 4.

Cover the ducks with the butter and lay the bacon over the breasts. Put a little water or stock in the bottom of a roasting tin or casserole. Place the ducks in the tin and cook for ¾ hour if young birds, if older cover the casserole or tin and cook for 1½ hours at a lower oven temperature.

Cook the washed blackberries in the orange juice for a few minutes, add the sugar and port, stir well and put to one side.

When the duck are cooked, remove the bacon, if the skin of the ducks is not brown return to the oven for a further 10 minutes. Remove from the oven and keep warm. Drain the fat from the juices in the tin. Pour the blackberry and port mixture into the juices, blend together. Season and add the lemon juice. Over a low heat reduce the liquid by ⅓. Pour over the duck or serve separately in a warm sauce boat. Serve with buttered peas, sautéd potatoes and an orange salad.

Venison Steaks with
Red Wine and Damson Sauce

All the Wiltshire forests once supplied fallow deer in large numbers to provide the monarch with venison. But deer were not always the main reason for hunting in the forests. Henry VIII found his third wife, Jane Seymour, in Savernake and would daily roam the forest in pursuit of his new love. Savernake, Selwood, Cranborne Chase and the New Forest all have increasing herds, mainly of fallow or roe deer, and their numbers are carefully controlled.

This particular recipe is an easy and delicious way to cook venison for a dinner party so you are not left slaving in the kitchen while your guests drink most of the wine!

TO SERVE FOUR

4 venison steaks
2 oz unsalted butter
2 tablespoons homemade damson jelly
Large wine glass of good red wine
2 tablespoons jellied stock
Salt and coarsely ground black pepper

Melt the butter in a heavy based frying pan or skillet. Fry the steaks according to taste, take care not to overcook or they will be very dry. Cook one or two steaks at a time over a high heat. Place onto a hot dish and keep warm.

Deglaze the pan with the red wine. Mix with the meat juices that are left in the pan. Add the damson jelly, jellied stock and the seasoning. Cook until reduced to a syrupy sauce, stir all the time, pour over the steaks and serve on a very hot dish with creamed potatoes, brussels sprouts and carrots. A large chunk of wholemeal bread to mop up the sauce would not go amiss.

PUDDINGS

Black Treacle Cream Mousse

Treacle is the syrup that remains after raw sugar has been crystallized; the blackest treacle is that which has had the most sugar removed, otherwise known as molasses. This mousse is easily one of the most popular sweets served in the restaurant. People have even threatened not to come to dinner if it is not on the menu! Although not strictly a Wiltshire recipe any cookery book of ours would not be complete without it.

3 eggs, separated
3 heaped tablespoons caster sugar
2 tablespoons water
2 tablespoons black treacle
10 fluid oz. whipping cream
3 teaspoons gelatine
2 oz chopped walnuts

Beat the egg yolks and sugar together until thick and ceamy, add the black treacle and the water, continue to beat for a further 2 minutes. Put the gelatine into a small bowl with 3 tablespoons of water and dissolve, resting the bowl over a suacepan of heated water, stir gently. When dissolved mix in well with the treacle mixture.

Whip the cream until the same consistency as the treacle mix and fold in about ¾ of it into the treacle, reserving the remainder for decoration. Whisk the egg whites until they hold their shape and fold into the mousse, mix well. Pour the mousse into a glass bowl or several small glasses and put into a cool place to set.

Serve with a rosette of cream and sprinkled with the chopped walnuts.

Christmas Plum Pudding

For the Christmas celebrations any fruit that was left in the larder was used for this magnificent pudding. The more mature the better, so plum puddings can be made months in advance. Store them in a dry well-ventilated place and steam a second time before serving.

2½ lb mixed fruit
1 lb soft dark sugar
1 teaspoon salt
¼ lb brazil nuts, chopped
½ lb dried apricots, chopped
4 oz carrot, grated and raw
1 lb apple grated
¾ lb brown wholemeal breadcrumbs
Grated rind and juice of 1 lemon
Grated rind and juice of 2 oranges
2 tablespoons malt or black treacle
4 large eggs
1 lb chopped suet
¼ pint milk
Small wine glass of brandy or rum

Put all the dry ingredients into a large container, including the fruit, apple and carrot.

Beat the eggs, malt or treacle, milk, rum or brandy, orange and lemon juice together in a jug. Pour this into the centre of the dry ingredients. Mix together thoroughly. Cover, and leave overnight.

Grease the insides of three one pound pudding basins, and place a small round of greaseproof paper on the bottom of each basin. Fill with the pudding mixture and cover the top with another round of greaseproof paper along with a double thickness of tin foil. Steam the puddings for 8 hours to produce a nice dark pudding.

On the day required steam the puddings for 3 hours. Turn out onto a warm serving dish, pour over a little warmed brandy or rum and set alight. Take to the table flaming and decorated with a small sprig of holly.

Serve with brandy butter, rum custard or sauce.

The Public Dinner in Salisbury Market Place to celebrate the coronation of Edward VII in 1902. 1,600 lbs of pudding were consumed.

Creed Wheat and Frumenty

Frumenty, firmenty, firmity, fromety, these are some of the variations on the name of one of England's oldest puddings. It was eaten on special occasions, Christmas Eve, harvest suppers, twelfth night, to celebrate sheep shearing, and, in Wiltshire, on Mothering Sunday or in mid-lent.

The wheat for frumenty is that which has been husked, hulled or pearled. It is polished in a special drum so that one layer of outer skin is rubbed off, and the ends of the grain nipped away. When it is cooked each grain swells into a soft ball suspended in a creamy jelly. Wholewheat grains, cracked, crushed or kibbled wheat can be used. These are obtainable from wholefood shops.

Frumenty is a very nourishing dish, hence Francis Kilvert's entry in his diary on Wednesday 29th March 1876; 'Visited William Pinnock the old blind man, and took from my mother a basin of Mid-Lent frumenty. He said he had only tasted it once in his life. He used when he was a ploughboy on a farm in Melksham Forest to be sent every Mothering Sunday with a jug of frumenty from Melksham Forest to a house in Lacock village'.

The day before, bring 1½ pints of milk to the boil and pour it over the wheat (8 oz). Put the milk and wheat into a pot or stoneware jar, with a lid, and leave it in a warm place (low oven, airing cupboard) to 'cree'. After 24 hours the wheat should have swollen and burst, and soaked up most of the milk turning the remainder to a thick jelly. If this has not happened, cook it gently until it turns, and allow to cool again. This is now 'creed' wheat ready to make into frumenty.

4 oz currants
2 oz sultanas
3 tablespoons rum or brandy
2 pints milk
3 beaten eggs
3 tablespoons honey
A little lemon peel

Grated nutmeg
Pinch cinnamon

Soak the fruit in the rum or brandy for several hours, add all the ingredients to the prepared wheat in a saucepan. Stir well and cook gently. The frumenty will become soft, thick and creamy. Extra honey and spices can be added if you wish. Serve either hot or cold with cream poured on top.

Country Treacle Tart

One icy cold Sunday, two winters ago, we were entertaining friends in our chapel restaurant. Eight of us sat down to a lunch of cream of Stilton soup, roast Pheasant, bacon rolls, bread sauce, roast potatoes, brussels sprouts, all with a damson and port sauce, and by special request, this treacle tart. That meal and the feeling of well-being, on a Sunday afternoon with the snow falling outside, log fire crackling in the stove, good friends and pleasant conversation, will remain with us for a long time. Two years, and many meals on, that memory lingers still each time we make this treacle tart.

6 oz shortcrust pastry
6 tablespoons golden syrup
2 oz fine, white breadcrumbs
Juice and grated rind of half a lemon

Line a pie dish with the rolled out pastry; warm the syrup in a pan and stir in the juice and grated rind of the lemon. Line the pastry case with the breadcrumbs, pour in the syrup mixture and cook at 375°F (190°C), gas mark 5 for 35 minutes.

It is best allow this pudding to cool a little or the treacle could burn the mouth.

Chilled Mulberry Soufflé

In 1610, James I ordered the mulberry tree to be planted to promote the growth of the silk weaving industry, the silk worm produces better silk if fed on the leaves of the white mulberry. Unfortunately for the worm and the industry, but luckily for us, the black mulberry was planted by mistake.

In the garden of our first restaurant at Wootton Bassett, we had a very ancient mulberry tree which each season produced so much fruit that we were able to make soufflés, ice-creams, mousses, cheesecakes, preserves, and serve plain but delicious mulberries and cream. If you can get a branch from someone's tree, and put it into the ground about a foot deep it has every chance of rooting, although it will grow very slowly and it will be a good few years before the tree will yield any fruit.

2 lb black mulberries
Grated rind and juice of 2 lemons
4 oz caster sugar
4 teaspoons gelatine
4 tablespoons water
½ pint double cream
4 large eggs

Prepare a 5 inch soufflé dish by tying a double thickness of greaseproof paper around the dish with at least 3 inches of paper above the rim. Secure with string tied very firmly. The soufflé will set above the rim giving it a 'risen' appearance.

Reserve some of the best mulberries for decorating and stew the remainder with the lemon rind and juice until the fruit is soft. When cooked, liquidize and pass through a fine sieve to remove the pips. Put to one side.

Separate the egg yolks from the white, beat the yolks with the sugar until very thick and creamy. Dissolve the gelatine in the water in a small bowl, and stand this bowl over hot water until completely clear.

Beat the mulberry purée into the egg yolk and sugar mixture, pour the gelatine into the purée in a steady stream, mix together well.

Beat half the quantity of double cream until it holds its shape and fold into the purée. Beat the egg whites, but not too much or they will not blend properly. Fold in the egg white, a third at a time, into the soufflé mixture. Do not over mix or you will lose the lightness. Pour the prepared soufflé into the dish and put into the refrigerator to set.

When it has set, beat the remainder of the cream and pipe with a large star nozzle onto the top of the soufflé. Decorate with the reserved mulberries. The fruit can be crystallized by dipping them into caster sugar before putting onto the soufflé.

Fresh Raspberry Fool

Wild raspberries have been known since the Bronze Age, and are one of our true native fruits. Raspberries began to be cultivated in gardens around the 15th-16th century. We are fortunate in having several wild raspberry bushes growing in the wood just beyond our restaurant, but this recipe is for those who have a glut of raspberries and would like a change from serving the fruit raw with cream.

1 lb fresh raspberries
¼ lb caster sugar
¼ pint redcurrant juice
½ pint double cream

Hull the berries and cook gently in the redcurrant juice until reduced to a pulp, add the sugar and stir until dissolved. Allow to cool.

Put the pulp through a sieve, stir in the cream and beat well. Pour into glasses and decorate with fresh raspberries. Chill before serving.

Devizes Cheesecake

For centuries cheese was one of Devizes's most important products. A soft curd cheese was made known as 'Little Wilts Cheese', which went into the making of the Devizes Cheese-cakes and were sold with the cheese at the monthly cheese markets. The original cheesecake recipe was as follows; 'to a pound and a half of cheese curd, put 10 oz of butter; beat both in a mortar until all looks like butter. Then add ¼ pound of almonds, beat fine with orange water, ¾ pound of sugar, 8 eggs, half ye whites, a little mace pounded and a little cream. Beat all together a quarter of an hour; bake in puff paste in a quick oven.'

This is our adapted recipe.

10 oz curd cheese
6 oz butter
4 oz ground almonds
4 oz caster sugar
3 eggs, plus 2 egg yolks
¼ teaspoon ground mace
2 tablespoons orange flower water
4 oz single cream
½ puff pastry or shortcrust

Line a 9 inch flan ring with the pastry and bake blind until it reaches a pale brown colour. Do not over cook as it has to be put into the oven again when cooking the cheesecake.

Cream the cheese and butter together, beat in the eggs, sugar, orange water, ground almonds and the mace. Heat the cream gently, and pour into the mixture, beat well together. Pour all into the cooked pastry case and cook for 35 minutes at 350°F (175°C), gas mark 4. Serve warm with fresh fruit and cream.

Dark Chocolate Pudding with Honey and Whisky Sauce

This rich, warming pudding was a great favourite in the days of our outside catering business, often appearing on the menu of the many shooting lunches that we used to do on the large estates of Wiltshire during autumn and winter.

1 oz cocoa powder
4 oz butter or margarine
2 eggs, beaten
4 oz caster sugar
a few drops of vanilla essence
a little milk to mix
6 oz self raising flour

FOR THE SAUCE
1 wine glass of whisky
½ pint of milk
4 tablespoons clear honey
Juice of two lemons
¼ pint double cream
1 heaped tablespoon cornflour

Half fill a large saucepan or steamer with water and put it on to boil; grease a 1½ pint pudding basin; cream together the sugar and butter or margarine until fluffy and pale. Add the beaten egg and vanilla essence a little at a time, beat well.

Make a smooth paste with the cocoa powder by adding a tablespoon of hot water. Pour this into the egg mixture.

Using a metal spoon, fold in half the flour that has been previously sifted, add enough milk to give a dropping consistency, fold in the remaining flour and a little extra milk to keep it to a smooth dropping consistency. Pour the mixture into the basin, cover with greaseproof paper and secure with string. Steam for 1½ hours.

To make the sauce; heat the ½ pint of milk gently, slacken the cornflour with a little cold water. Add the honey and the corn-flour to the hot milk, stir well until it thickens. Pour in the whisky and lemon juice, stir well. Then gently beat in the cream.

Pour the sauce over the hot chocolate pudding when ready to serve, or serve separately in a warm jug.

Fleur's Brandy Junket

Fleur, our Golden Guernsey goat, supplies our milk twice daily, and when we have a glut we make cottage cheese or this deli-cious junket. With the addition of brandy, it makes a traditional nursery pudding into something a little more interesting.

1 pint fresh milk
Nutmeg, grated
1 tablespoon soft, brown sugar
1 teaspoon rennet
2 tablespoons brandy (can be omitted if serving to children)

Heat the milk to blood heat, 98°F, unless you have a goat or even a dairy cow, in which case use fresh from milking, strained in the usual way. The heat can be tested by dipping your fingers into the milk, it must not be allowed to get too hot. When the correct temperature has been reached, remove from the heat and add the sugar, rennet and brandy. Pour into a glass bowl or individual glasses, dust the top with the grated nutmeg. It will take about 5 minutes to set if the weather is warm, a little longer in winter. Serve after a rich main course, or as an alternative to a sweet pudding.

Fresh Orange Cheesecake

Cheesecakes were one of the earliest forms of puddings — curd and soft cheese being made in abundance from the surplus milk of Wiltshire's many dairies.

8 oz digestive biscuits
3 oz unsalted butter
¼ pint milk
8 oz cottage cheese
2 oz caster sugar
Grated rind and juice of 1 lemon
Grated rind and juice of 2 oranges
½ pint double cream
3 teaspoons gelatine
2 egg whites

Break the biscuits and put into a blender, mix until well broken into crumbs. Put the biscuit crumbs into a bowl. Melt the butter and pour over the biscuit, mix well together.

Put the milk, sugar, cheese, lemon rind, orange rind, and the fruit juices into a blender, mix until smooth. Pour into a separate bowl.

Dissolve the gelatine in a small dish, placed in a saucepan with a little boiling water, then add it to the lemon and orange mixture. Beat the cream until it is firm and fold it into the fruit mixture. Beat the egg whites (do not over beat) and fold into the fruit mixture.

Press the biscuit crumbs firmly onto the base of a loose sided cake tin, allow to set for a few minutes before adding the cheese and orange mixture. Put into a refrigerator to set.

When ready, decorate with a little whipped cream piped on in rosettes, and fresh orange segments around the edge of the cake.

Pear Caramel

'From your chamber window, when you rise in the morning, you may put out your hand and take more bunches of the same fruit that is from the left side of the window; if you come in the Autumn and look out of the right side, there will hang great, ripe pears for your breakfast.'

So wrote Richard Jefferies in *Landscape and Labour*. The pear, and the Bramley apple, are the two most commonly planted trees in the cottage garden. We buy our pears at the twice-weekly Marlborough market. Buy those that are firm and keep them in the kitchen until they are ripe. A ripe pear gives very slightly around the stem, but should not be at all squashy.

When cooking pears it is a good idea to add some lemon juice to prevent them from turning brown.

Ripe pears, peeled and quartered
(as many as you have people to eat them)
Whipped cream
Coarse brown sugar
Lemon juice

Put the prepared pears into an ovenproof dish, sprinkle with the lemon juice. Spread the whipped cream over the pears and chill for several hours. When required, sprinkle over the brown sugar and put under the grill to caramelize.

Totter Pie (Raised Apple Pie)

Totter is an old word for anything raised. On the Marlborough Downs, just a mile from where we live, is a place called Totterdown. It is now part of a nature reserve and has a small lake and a derelict shepherd's cottage. It is situated on the summit of a ridge overlooking the rest of the reserve and part of Devil's Den. Totter was the local name given to this pie because of its tall, raised pastry case.

FOR THE PASTRY
1½ lb self raising flour
Generous pinch of salt
½ lb lard
¼ pint milk and water mixed
1 egg
3 oz caster sugar

FOR THE FILLING
2 lb apples, peeled and sliced
4 oz granulated sugar
Juice of half a lemon
Melted crab apple jelly (page 119)

Sift the flour and salt together in a large bowl, rub in half the quantity of lard. Boil the remaining lard with the milk and water. When it is boiling, pour into the centre of the flour and stir well. Beat the egg and sugar together, and add to the flour mixture. Knead the pastry and leave to stand for a few minutes to let the pastry 'rest'. Line a raised pie mould, or raise the pastry around a large jam jar, then tie a double piece of greaseproof paper round it, then carefully remove the jar.

Fill the pastry shell with the sliced apple. Sprinkle the lemon juice and sugar over the apple as you pack it. Take care not to push the apple through the pastry. Place a lid made from any left-over pastry from the case on top of the pie and seal with a little beaten egg or milk. Make a hole in the top to allow the steam to escape and for adding the crab apple jelly later. Bake for

20 minutes at 400°F (200°C), gas mark 6, then lower the heat to 350°F (180°C), gas mark 4 and continue to cook for a further 1½ hours. When the pie is cooked and has been allowed to cool a little, melt the crab apple jelly and pour into the pie through the hold in the lid. Leave until cold and firm before eating. Serve with a large jug of pouring cream.

This is a perfect pudding for picnics.

Wyndham's Dairy, Salisbury.

Treacle Bolly (a treacle pudding)

The Kennet River runs through the grounds of Marlborough College and from it, by a wooded bank, stem five or six clear pools known as Treacle Bolly Springs. The footpath running parallel to the river takes its name from the springs. It is a muddy path at the best of times but after rain it turns into a tacky, sticky mire. Noting the likeness, the boys named this pudding after that swampy footpath. It is still made today and a few years ago a special Treacle Bolly Pudding was made for an old Marlburian reunion.

½ lb plain flour
4 oz suet
1 oz breadcrumbs
Grated rind of ½ lemon
Black treacle (golden syrup can be used if you prefer)
½ teaspoon baking powder
Pinch of salt

Mix together the flour, suet, baking powder and salt, form into a stiff paste with cold water. Divide the paste into two equal portions; with one portion line a basin, from the other, cut off sufficient paste to form a lid, roll the remainder out thinly.

Put a layer of treacle in the basin and sprinkle with breadcrumbs. Sprinkle over a little lemon rind.

From the rolled out paste cut a round large enough to cover the treacle and breadcrumbs in the basin; moisten the edges with water and join it carefully to the paste lining the basin. Now add another layer of treacle, breadcrumbs and lemon rind, cover as before. Repeat until the basin is full, then cover with a layer of greaseproof paper, then a layer of foil, seal well around the rim. Steam for 2½ hours.

Quince and Pumpkin Flan

Each autumn, Ivy Bagwell, our 'vegetable lady', who not only prepares them, but who with husband, Charlie, also grows them, harvest giant pumpkins. Like the pumpkin, quinces have been around for hundreds of years. The ancient Greeks called them 'golden apples' and regarded them as a symbol of love and happiness. In Tudor times quince was used as a spiced jelly to accompany meat, or as a filling for tarts. Pumpkin and quince, both having a delicate flavour, mingle perfectly to make a very different but delicious pudding.

1 lb quince flesh
6 teaspoons gelatine
3 tablespoons cold water
4 oz caster sugar
Juice and grated rind of 1 large orange
2 eggs, separated
1 lb pumpkin flesh
½ lb digestive biscuits
3 oz unsalted butter
¾ pint whipping cream

Peel and remove the skin and pips from the pumpkin, place the flesh in a saucepan with a little water to cover the bottom to prevent sticking. Peel, core and slice the quince, add to the pumpkin, cook gently until both are soft. Add the sugar, grated orange rind and the juice to the fruit, liquidize to a purée.

Add the egg yolks to the purée one at a time, liquidize for a couple of seconds between each yolk, make sure they are blended in well.

Crush the digestive biscuits finely, melt the butter slowly, then mix into the crushed biscuit. Press the biscuit mixture into the bottom of a ten inch loose sided cake tin, and place in the refrigerator to set.

Dissolve the gelatine in the 3 tablespoons of water by standing a bowl which contains the gelatine in a saucepan of hot water until the gelatine has completely melted. Add this to the fruit purée, stir in well.

Whisk ½ pint of the cream and add to the fruit mixture, reserve the remainder for decoration.

Whisk the egg whites and fold them carefully into the fruit purée, pour into the cake tin and leave to set in a cool place.

Prune and Brandy Mousse

This simple pudding is a good stand-by, as most kitchens contain at least one packet of dried prunes, and with the addition of brandy and cream, schoolday images of prunes and custard will hopefully fade.

1 lb large prunes
½ pint water
¼ pint brandy
4 tablespoons caster sugar
3 teaspoons gelatine
½ pint double cream

Soak the prunes with the water and brandy for at least 24 hours until soft and swollen. When soft, remove the stones. Liquidize the prunes and sugar together, any liquid left in the soaking bowl pour into the liquidizer with the prunes. When the mixture is smooth, turn out into a bowl.

Moisten the gelatine in 4 tablespoons of water (cold) in a small basin. Stand the basin in a pan of hot water to dissolve the gelatine. When completely dissolved, add to the prune mixture and stir thoroughly.

Whip the cream and fold ⅔ into the mousse reserving the other ⅓ for decoration. Chill thoroughly and decorate with rosettes of whipped cream.

Summer Pudding

Summer pudding was a way of using up any stale, surplus bread and adding soft fruit to make it edible. Nowadays it is so popular that it has become a pudding in its own right with ingredients bought specially. Most soft fruits can be used but go easy on the blackcurrants or blackberries if you use them, they will make the pudding too dark in colour.

Summer pudding is best prepared the day before it is needed.

1 large white loaf (not sliced) cut into slices ½ inch thickness
1 lb redcurrants
1 lb raspberries
1 lb strawberries
½ lb blackcurrants
½ lb caster sugar

2 one pound pudding basins

Remove the crust from the bread and cut into thick slices. Ideally the bread should be about one week old, as if fresh it will be too moist to absorb the fruit juices. Line the basins with the bread slices making sure there are no gaps between the slices. Reserve a few slices to top the puddings when completed. Prepare and wash the fruit, reserve a few for decoration and place in a heavy-based saucepan.

Heat the fruit gently until the juices begin to run, then add the sugar, stir well. When the sugar has dissolved, take off the heat and spoon the fruit ito the basins, making sure the fruit is evenly distributed. Top with the remaining slices of bread then place a saucer on top of the bread and weigh down with a suitable heavy object. Allow to cool, then refrigerate for at least 24 hours before serving to allow the juice to soak into the bread.

When required, turn the puddings out of the basins onto a dish, decorate with the reserved fruit dipped into sugar. Serve with lots of cream.

Note: If after 24 hours in the refrigerator you wish to freeze the pudding, remove the weight and cover the top of the pudding with foil or greaseproof paper. Also, plastic basins are best as you are able to see if any of the bread needs more juice. This can be added by gently pulling away the bread from the side of the bowl using a palette knife, and pouring in any juice which you may have left over. Summer puddings freeze very well.

Strawberries in Elderflower Syrup

Major and Mrs Martin Gibbs, who live at Sheldon Manor, make this delicious syrup when elderflowers are in season. They have kindly passed the recipe on to us, but if you would like to sample it before making it, it is to be found on the menu during the summer months in their 17th century converted stable block restaurant in the grounds of the Manor.

1 lb sugar and 1 pint of water boiled for 1 minute. Remove from the heat and add a good handful of elderflowers. After 4 hours strain off the elderflowers and store the syrup.

This is quite delicious poured over strawberries half-an-hour before serving.

Victorian Plum Sorbet

This refreshing sorbet is a good way to use up any surplus plums.

1 lb Victoria Plums
½ lb caster sugar
½ pint cold water
Juice of 1 lemon

Stone the plums and cook them slowly with a little water to stop the fruit sticking to the bottom of the pan. Heat the ½ pint of water with the sugar until it turns to a sugar syrup. Put to one side. Liquidize the cooked plums to a purée, then pass through a sieve into a bowl, add the lemon juice and sugar syrup, stir well. Check the taste in case you would like to add a little more sugar or lemon juice. Put into a container and freeze.

When the sorbet is half frozen, take out of the freezer and stir well, this breaks up any ice crystals that will have formed.

Vanilla Ice-cream

6 egg yolks
4 oz sugar
1 pint single cream
2 teaspoons vanilla sugar to 12 drops vanilla essence

Beat the egg yolks and sugar together until thick and creamy. Rinse a small pan with cold water and heat the cream with the vanilla flavouring. When it is nearly boiling, pour slowly into the egg mixture, still beating.

Place the bowl over a pan of simmering water (or use a double saucepan) and stir the mixture until it begins to thicken. Allow to cool. Freeze in suitable containers.

Remove from the freezer an hour before serving. Leave in the refrigerator.

Lorries at Wilts United Dairies, Wootton Bassett, in about 1922.

Blackberry Ice-cream

Ice-cream became popular with the advent of ice-houses that were built in the grounds of country estates in the 18th century. They were deep, brick-lined pits, covered with brick and stone-work domes, and the ice would be taken from local lakes, canals or ponds. If the winter was not cold enough locally, ice would be brought from the Fens or the Lake District in waggons insulated with straw. The records show that one of the first ice-creams to be made was a fruit flavoured cream, poured into a tin and kept in a bucket of ice.

1 lb blackberries
5 oz sugar
½ pint double cream
¼ pint water

Blend the blackberries into a purée and strain them through a sieve. Boil the sugar and the water over a moderate heat for 3 minutes and allow to cool. Stir the sugar syrup into the black-berry purée and allow to cool, then gently fold in the lightly whipped double cream. Freeze into a suitable container.

Remove from the freezer about an hour before serving and leave in the refrigerator. Decorate with a few crystallized black-berries (fruit dipped in sugar).

SAUCES

Béchamel Sauce

To make ½ pint of Sauce

½ small onion
½ pint milk
½ bay leaf
¼ teaspoon grated nutmeg
1 oz plain flour
Sprig of thyme
1 oz unsalted butter
3 tablespoons single cream
Salt and black pepper

Put the milk with the bay leaf, onion, thyme, nutmeg into a pan and bring gently to the boil. Remove from the heat, cover and leave the milk to infuse for 15 minutes. In a clean heavy-based pan, melt the butter, stir in the flour and cook for 3 minutes.

Strain the milk through a fine sieve and blend it into the roux. Bring to the boil stirring all the time, then simmer for 2-3 minutes. Adjust the seasoning and stir in the cream.

Caper Sauce

In the middle of the 17th century, capers were being imported from southern Europe. If these could not be obtained, pickled broom buds were used instead. Today we use 'English' capers or pickled nasturtium seeds.

1 oz butter
1 oz plain flour
½ pint mutton, lamb or chicken stock
¼ pint single cream
2 dessertspoons capers
1 dessertspoon chopped parsley
Lemon juice to taste
Salt and black pepper

Melt the butter in a saucepan, add the flour and cook for 2-3 minutes stirring continuously until you have a 'roux'. Remove from the heat and gradually add the heated stock, stir all the time until smooth and creamy. Return to the heat and bring to the boil then simmer for 5 minutes, stirring ocasionally. Add the parsley, capers, lemon juice, salt and pepper, stir in the cream last of all. Serve hot with the mutton patties or roast lamb.

Home-made Mayonnaise

2 egg yolks
½ teaspoon made mustard
3 tablespoons wine vinegar(white)
½ pint olive oil
Salt and white pepper

Put the mustard into the bottom of a bowl, add the egg yolks and whisk lightly. Pour on the oil drop by drop. This must be done very slowly, stirring constantly. The mayonnaise will thicken until almost solid by the time the oil has been added. Season to taste and stir in the vinegar, using sufficient to give the required consistency.

Should the mayonnaise curdle it is because the oil has been added too quickly, in which case, break another egg yolk into a clean bowl and add the curdled mixture slowly. More oil must be added to compensate for the extra egg yolk. If the mayonnaise becomes too stiff during preparation a little vinegar will thin it down.

Plum Sauce

Fruit sauces became popular during the Edwardian era. They combine well with cold meats, game and poultry. The piquant flavour of the plum blends well with spices. Victoria or yellow plums give a golden-brown hue to the sauce particularly if white vinegar is used instead of malt. Damsons can also be used if you prefer.

TO MAKE ABOUT 1½ PINTS

2 lb Victoria or yellow plums
8 oz sugar
1 pint white wine vinegar
1 teaspoon salt
½ teaspoon cayenne pepper
10 cloves
1 teaspoon ground ginger
1 teaspoon finely chopped mint

Wash the plums and chop them into pieces, put them into a large, heavy-based pan with their stones. Add all the other ingredients, stir over a gentle heat until the sugar has dissolved, then bring rapidly to the boil.

Reduce the heat and simmer for 30 minutes, stirring occasionally. Then push the mixture through a sieve. When well sieved, return the fruit purée to a clean pan and simmer for 40 minutes, stir from time to time until the sauce has the consistency of thick cream. Bottle and seal in the usual way.

Keep for about a month before using.

PRESERVES

Apple Chutney

A well made chutney should have a fairly smooth texture and a mellow flavour. They have long added interest to cold meats, patés, casseroles, bread and cheese and salads. They are also a good way of using up damaged fruit as long as the bruised part is cut away.

4 lb apples, peeled and cored
1 lb onions, peeled and sliced
½ lb sultanas or dates, chopped
1½ lb Demerara sugar
4 teaspoons salt
2 teaspoons ground mixed spice
2 teaspoons ground ginger
1 level teaspoon cayenne pepper
1½ pints white vinegar

Chop the apples and put them into a large pan with the onion, fruit, spices and seasoning. Cover with a little water and cook until soft. This is to prevent the fruit from sticking. When the fruit is soft, add the vinegar and sugar, simmer until it has thickened. Put into clean, warm jars, allow to cool before sealing.

Apple Marmalade

Good flavoured eating apples
(any you do not use can always be eaten)
1 lb granulated sugar to each pint of apple purée

Wipe the apples and cut into quarters. Place in a large pan, add just sufficient water to cover the apples, cook slowly until reduced to a pulp. Put the sugar and apple pulp into a clean pan and cook together until you have a jam-like consistency, at this stage it should be fairly thick. Put into hot clean jars and allow to cool, then cover.

Bramble Jelly

Blackberries are the most plentiful of our wild fruit, and the most versatile – for they can be added to pies, tarts, game, jams, jellies or wine. This jelly will go equally well with duck, pheasant, partridge, rabbit, as well as spread thickly on homemade scones.

4 lb blackberries
¾ pint water
Sugar
Juice of 2 lemons

Thoroughly wash the blackberries removing any bits. Put them with the lemon juice and water into a pan and simmer for 1 hour, or until the fruit is soft and pulpy. Strain through a jelly cloth, measure the fruit purée and return it to the pan with 1 lb of sugar to each pint of purée. Stir until the sugar has dissolved and boil rapidly until a 'jell' is obtained. Skim. Pot and cover in the usual way.

Crab Apple Jelly

Crab apples were used in medieval times for making a type of vinegar called verjuice. They were much in use until lemons and limes becams fashionable. Made into a jelly, they make the perfect accompaniment to cold meats, game and meaty patés.

6 lb crab apples
Juice of 1 lemon
Granulated sugar, 1 lb to every pint of liquid

Wash the apples, remove any stalks, cut into quarters and put into a large pan, add the lemon juice and about 4 pints of water. Simmer gently until soft, then strain through a jelly bag or sieve. Measure the apple liquid and to each pint add 1 lb sugar.

Put the apple juice and sugar into a pan and cook on a moderate heat stirring all the time until the sugar has dissolved, then boil rapidly until the temperature increases to 220°F (110°C) which is setting point. Allow to cool then put into hot, clean jars and seal.

Elderberry Jelly

The elder tree has as many virtues as it has superstitions attached to it. Gypsies regard it as an unlucky tree to camp under; yet there is an old saying that claims it to be the safest tree to shelter under during a storm as it is never struck by lightning. You must never burn elder, so another saying goes, for 'you burn your luck if you burn elderwood'. It is also said that if you cut an elder and it bleeds, then it is a witches' tree, for witches were believed to often turn into elder and were sometimes unable to reverse the process. Whatever the stories it is certainly most useful, providing young buds for salads and flowers and berries for jam and wine.

2 lb cooking apples
2 lb elderberries
1 pint water
Sugar

Wash the elderberries and apples. Chop the apples roughly without peeling or coreing. Cook the fruit separately with just enough water to cover. Simmer until soft and pulpy. Strain the fruit through a jelly bag, measure the purée and return both fruits to the same pan with ¾ lb of sugar to each pint of purée. Stir until the sugar has dissolved. Boil rapidly until you have a 'jell'. Skim, pot and cover in the usual way.

Elderberry Wine

Making country wines did not become popular until the 17th century when sugar became more plentiful and consequently cheaper. The addition of blackberries to this elderberry wine makes it a very rich, almost port-like wine. Excellent for warming one up on a cold, winter's evening when sipped by a roaring fire. It is also very good for cooking if you have sufficient to spare.

TO MAKE ONE GALLON

Port style yeast
2 lb elderberries, stripped from stalks
½ lb sloes
1 lb blackberries
Juice and rind of 1 lemon
2 lb sugar

Boil sloes in 1 quart of water to soften, put the rest of the fruit into a bin and crush, add the sloes and the rest of the boiling water. Stir well once or twice a day for 5-7 days.

Strain off the pulp and boil the liquor with the rind of the lemon for 20 minutes, return to the bin, add the juice of the lemon and the 2 lbs of sugar. If you prefer a sweeter wine, the sugar can be increased to 3 lbs when the first fermentation is completed.

Add a port style yeast when the liquid has cooled, following the directions on the packet.

Put the wine into a demijohn and fit airlock, any surplus can be put into a bottle for topping up later. Be sure to use an airlock or plug neck with cotton wool.

When fermentation ceases, rack off into clean jars and leave for 6-12 months in a cool place. Tasting will tell if it is ready or requires more sugar. Elderberry wine sometimes takes 2-3 years to mature, by adding sloes and blackberries, it appears to speed up the process.

Damson Cheese

Damson cheese is really a jelly and is not like cheese at all. It is a splendid accompaniment to roast lamb or venison, can be eaten stirred in junket or milk puddings, or spread on bread and butter. It is much firmer than curd or jam and is served in slices or wedges. Pot in a mould or wide-mouthed jars so that it can be easily turned out.

TO MAKE 3-4 LBS
6 lb damsons
½ pint water
Sugar

Wash the fruit and remove any stems, put into a large pan with the water. Bring to the boil, then cover and simmer gently until the fruit is tender, about 30 minutes. Pass the pulp through a nylon sieve, then weigh the purée. After weighing, put the fruit into a clean pan with the sugar, allowing 1 lb sugar to each 1 lb of fruit. Stir until the sugar has dissolved, bring to the boil quickly, then simmer gently for 45 minutes to 1 hour until thick. Stir frequently to prevent the fruit from sticking. The cheese is ready when a wooden spoon is drawn across the top and it leaves a clear line. After potting it takes at least 2 months to mature.

Mint Jelly

Ideal for cold meat especially roast lamb. Rosemary jelly can be made in the same way using 4 tablespoons of fresh leaves in place of the mint.

3 lb cooking apples
1 lb sugar to each pint of juice
2 heaped tablespoons finely chopped mint
4 tablespoons white vinegar

If you think it necessary, a couple of drops of green food colouring to each pound of sugar can be added.

Cut the apples and core, do not peel. Put into a large pan and cover them with water, bring to the boil and simmer until reduced to a pulp, strain through a jelly bag.

Put the apple pulp along with the sugar and vinegar into a large pan, dissolve the sugar over a low heat, stir gently. When all the sugar is dissolved, raise the heat and boil until the temperature reaches 220°F (110°C). When the required temperature has been reached, take off the heat, allow to cool and put into warm, clean jars, seal.

Muscat-Gooseberry Jam

Gooseberries grow quite early on in the year, and are a very popular combination with oily fish, and goose (from which it does not derive its name). They are made into fools, sauces, jellies, put into meringues and as here made into jam. The muscat sweetness of the elderflowers make this jam a welcome addition to the tea table. The early, small green gooseberries have the better flavour for cooking. The scent of the elderflower is very strong so be careful not to exceed the recommended number of flower heads or it will overpower the flavour of the gooseberries.

FOR ABOUT 10 LBS JAM
4½ lbs gooseberries
1½ pints of water
12-14 heads of elderflowers
6 lbs sugar

Wash, top and tail the gooseberries, put into a large pan with the water. Put the elderflower heads into a muslin bag, secure with string and place the bag into the pan with the gooseberries. Simmer for 30 minutes until the fruit is soft, then mash the fruit to a pulp, add the sugar, stir from time to time until it has all dissolved. Bring the jam rapidly to the boil until setting point is reached. Remove the elderflower bag and discard. Allow the jam to cool slightly and pot in clean warm jars.

Sweet Spiced Apple

Another delicious and simple recipe from the nuns of Abbey House in Malmesbury. It can be used as a pie filling or served with ice-cream.

8 lbs apples, peeled, cored, and chopped
½ pint water
½ pint white wine vinegar

Mix these ingredients together and leave to stand overnight.

5 lb granulated sugar
12 cloves tied in muslin (optional)

Put all ingredients into a large pan and bring to the boil for 45 minutes, stir often to prevent burning. When ready, bottle in warm, clean, screw-top jars. If sealed well will lay for several years.

BREAD AND
CAKES

'MARLBOROUGH'

Here comes Muffin-man down the street,
With trays and baize and bell,
Calling and bawling and shuffling his feet,
And carrying muffins as well.

Muffin man: Muffin man: Little you'll say
The smart my heart must know,
At seeing, and fleeing unwilling, away
From the muffins I long for so.

Muffin oh; Muffins oh; Time was when
(How glad, yet sad, to say)
Greedy, and needy, I gobbled up ten
And practic'lly passed away.

Muffin man: Muffin man: Saying to me:
(I know your low design)
"Stop fretting, forgetting the pains to be".
All right, I'll purchase nine.

from *Betjeman Country* compiled by Frank Delaney

Muffins

In the 19th century muffins reached the height of their popularity, due to the muffin man who toured the streets with his loaded tray of hot muffins balanced upon his head. When splitting muffins, they must be pulled apart and never cut with a knife, as cutting them makes them doughy.

TO MAKE ABOUT 12

1 lb strong plain flour
1 egg
½ pint milk
1 teaspoon salt
1 oz butter
½ oz fresh yeast
1 teaspoon sugar

Put the butter and milk into a saucepan and warm to blood heat, break in the egg and beat well together.

Cream the yeast and sugar together with about 4 tablespoons of water that has been slightly warmed. Put the flour into a warm bowl and make a well in the centre, pour in the yeast, then add the egg and butter mixture. Knead well together, add a little more warm water if needed. The dough should be soft but not sticky. Cover the dough with a cloth and leave in a warm place for about 1½ hours until the dough has doubled in size. After it has risen, knead again lightly and then roll out to ½ inch thickness on a floured board. Cut out the muffins with a large scone cutter or knife, roughly 2½ inches across. Knead the trimmings together and repeat the process. Leave them to rise again in a warm place for 35-40 minutes.

Heat a griddle, frying pan or cooking tray, lightly oiled, lift on the dough pieces 3-4 at a time, and cook over a medium heat for 6 minutes on either side. They should rise quite dramatically and retain their floury look. Toast them by the fire, pull apart and spread generously with butter.

Crumpets

'She who eats her greasy crumpets snugly in the inglenook of some birch-enshrouded homestead, dropping butter on her book!' What a wonderful description John Betjeman gives of these deliciously light, spongy tea-cakes. In the winter we make crumpets at least once a week. Spread generously with butter and homemade jam. They are also good for breakfast with fried bacon and a fried egg topping the crumpet. Crumpet rings are available from any good kitchen shop. We buy ours from 'Kitchens' of Bath. Alternatively a large, plain pastry cutter can be used. In both cases the rings must be well greased. The size of the rings are about 4 inches in diameter.

20-24 CRUMPETS
1½ lb plain flour
¾ oz live yeast
1 teaspoon salt
1¾ pints of milk

Grease the crumpet rings, sift the flour with the salt into a warm bowl. Heat the milk until lukewarm and dissolve the yeast in ¼ pint of the milk. Make a well in the centre of the flour and pour in the milk and yeast, stir well. Add the remainder of the milk until a batter is formed, the consistency of cream. Cover, and leave for 40-45 minutes to allow the mixture to rise.

Set the crumpet rings onto a hot, greased griddle or baking sheet, or a large frying pan. Pour the batter into the rings, fill to about ½ inch. Cook for 3-4 minutes until brown then turn the crumpet over and cook the other side. Crumpets can also be cooked in the oven; pre-set at 375°F (190°C), gas mark 5, cook for 20-25 minutes.

The crumpets must not be too brown as they must be toasted before eating.

Honey Flap-Jacks

Honey was the earliest form of sweetening. The ancient Greeks believed that it promoted health and long life. Whether this be true or not, it is a most marvellous aid to cooking and we use it prolifically in the restaurant. Our honey comes from hives in the Pewsey Vale and is bought from the local W.I. Market on Saturdays mornings in Marlborough High Street.

6 oz butter or margarine
6 oz brown sugar
8 oz rolled oats
2 tablespoons clear honey
Pinch of salt

Put the oats, salt and sugar together into a mixing bowl; melt the butter or margarine over a low heat and add the honey. When melted, pour onto the oat mixture and mix well together.

Grease a baking tray, one with sides if you have one, press the mixture evenly into the tray. Cook in the oven for ½ hour until golden brown at 350°F (175°C), gas mark 4.

When ready, remove from the oven and cut into squares, cool the flap-jacks before storing them in an air tight container.

Malted Wholemeal Bread

We use only organically grown flour which is entirely free from modern fertilizers. It can be bought from the Rushall Farm Mill, near Pewsey, where you can also buy their home-baked bread. The addition of malt makes this bread even more delicious and is a great favourite in the restaurant.

1 lb strong white flour
1 lb wholemeal flour
1 level dessert-spoon caster sugar
1 level dessert-spoon salt
1 oz fresh yeast
2 tablespoons vegetable oil
1 tablespoon brewers malt
1 pint warm water

In a large bowl, mix the flour, salt and sugar together. Crumble the yeast and add a little warm water to form a smooth paste; add half of the remaining water to the yeast paste, along with the malt and oil. Mix well together, pour into the centre of the flour mixture. Blend together then add the remainder of the water, mix until you have a smooth, elastic dough.

Turn onto a work surface and knead for 5 minutes. Put into a clean bowl and cover with a greased polythene bag, leave to rise for 2 hours in a warm place. Turn out and knead again to remove any air bubbles.

Shape the dough into loaves or rolls, put onto a greased tray, cover and leave to rise for a further 35 minutes. Cook in a very hot oven: 40 minutes for loaves, 20 minutes for rolls.

Spread generously with butter; this bread is almost a meal in itself.

Rich Chocolate Cake

Although Britain possessed chocolate in the 17th century, it was used mainly as a breakfast drink, although one or two recipes existed for making chocolate sweetmeats, but they were very time consuming and laborious. The first elegant chocolates were produced by the French and by the middle of the 18th century chocolate could be bought in England in slabs or daintily shaped with a variety of fillings.

1 teaspoon bicarbonate of soda
4 oz cooking fat (e.g. Trex or Cookeen)
10 oz caster sugar
2 eggs, beaten
6 oz plain flour
¼ teaspoon baking powder
Pinch of salt
2 oz cocoa
7½ fluid oz cold water

FOR THE FILLING

15 fluid oz double cream
Icing sugar to taste

Beat the cooking fat and sugar together until the mixture is light and fluffy and then whisk in the beaten eggs, a little at a time. Sift the flour with the baking powder, salt and bicarbonate of soda, stir into the fat and sugar mixture. Mix the cocoa and water to a paste and add to the flour and sugar mixture. Beat until all the ingredients are thoroughly incorporated, pour into a greased 10 inch loose-sided cake tin lined with lightly greased grease-proof paper. Bake for 1 hour until the cake begins to come away from the sides of the tin. Cool on a wire rack, then split in half using a sharp knife.

To make the filling: whip the cream until it just holds its shape, gradually add the icing sugar to taste, blend well. Spread on one side of the cake rounds and sandwich the two together.

The cake can be iced if you wish with 8 oz icing sugar, 2 tablespoons of cocoa and enough hot water to make a paste beaten until smooth. Cover the top of the cake, spreading smoothly and evenly.

If you wish to have a rich chocolate pudding after a dinner or lunch party, this cake would adapt very well with whipped cream rosettes around the edge of the cake, chocolate leaves and/or chocolate shavings (a potato peeler is good for shaving chocolate from a slab) and a fresh rose (not too big) in the centre.

Hot Teacakes

7 oz flour
3 oz sugar
3 oz unsalted butter
1 dessertspoon baking powder
2 eggs
Pinch of salt
5 fluid ozs milk

Rub the butter into the flour, add the sugar, salt and baking powder. Whisk the eggs and mix with the milk, then add to the flour mixture.

Stir well with a fork and put into a buttered baking tin, bake for ½ hour in a hot oven. When cooked, turn out of the tin, split open, butter and serve at once.

Wiltshire Lardy Cake

Lard being the most widely available cooking fat in the days when nearly every household kept a pig, it was only natural to use lard in the place of butter, which was considerably more expensive. In true Wiltshire style, nothing was ever wasted, so at the end of the baking day, using any left-over dough, Lardy cake came into being. It is very fattening, but it was intended to be a filling and substantial food in an age of low wages and widespread poverty.

1 lb bread dough which has risen for an hour
and doubled in bulk
6 oz mixed dried fruit
6 oz lard
6 oz granulated sugar
2 oz mixed peel

Roll out the dough into an oblong, spread two-thirds of it with one third each of lard, fruit, peel and sugar. Fold into three. Press the ends down together with a rolling pin, and give the dough a half turn. Repeat this twice more.

Place the folded dough into a large square or oblong tin which allows enough room for it to rise. Leave in a warm, draught-free place for 20-30 minutes, then bake at 425°F (220°C), gas mark 7 for about 45 minutes. Take out of the oven, then put onto a plate, upside down, the sugary side uppermost. Lardy cake is best eaten warm from the oven and cut into generous, sticky squares.

BIBLIOGRAPHY

The Natural History of Wiltshire, John Aubrey
Portrait of Wiltshire, Pamela Street
Wiltshire Rhymes, Edward Slow
Talking of John Austen, Sheila Kaye-Smith and G.B. Stern
Field and Hedgerow, Richard Jefferies
Wiltshire Miscellany, J.A. Leete
Tales of Old Wiltshire, Cecilia Millson
Martin Chuzzlewit, Charles Dickens
The Book of Household Management, Mrs Beeton
The Victoria History of Wiltshire (vols. III, IV)
The Letters of Jane Austen, edited by R.W. Chapman
English Food, Jane Grigson
The Collected Poems, John Betjeman
Betjeman Country, Frank Delaney
English Cookery New and Old, Susan Campbell
Farmhouse Cookery

The publishers would like to thank The Wiltshire Library & Museum Service, The Wiltshire Natural History & Archaeological Society, and The Salisbury & South Wiltshire Museum for their assistance in providing the photographs that illustrate the recipes.

METRIC CONVERSION TABLES

British	Metric
16 oz (1 lb)	450 g
8 oz (½ lb)	225 g
4 oz (¼ lb)	100 g
1 oz	25 g

Metric
1000 grammes (g) = 1 kilogramme (kilo)

Metric	British
1 kilo (1000 g)	2 lb 3 oz
½ kilo (500 g)	2 lb 2 oz
¼ kilo (250 g)	9 oz
100 g	4 oz

LIQUID MEASURES
(approximate equivalents)

Metric
1 litre = 10 decilitres (dl) = 100 centilitres (cl) = 1000 millilitres (ml)

British	Metric
1 quart	1.1 litres
1 pint	6 dl
½ pint	3 dl
¼ pint	1.5 dl
1 tablespoon	15 ml
1 dessertspoon	10 ml
1 teaspoon	5 ml

Metric	British
1 litre	35 fluid oz
½ litre (5 dl)	18 fluid oz
¼ litre (2.5 dl)	9 fluid oz
1 dl	4 fluid oz

DOMESTIC OVEN TEMPERATURES

	Electric (F°)	Celsius (C°)	Gas
Very cool	225	110	¼
Very cool	250	130	½
Cool	275	140	1
Cool	300	150	2
Warm	325	170	3
Moderate	350	180	4
Fairly hot	375	190	5
Fairly hot	400	200	6
Hot	425	220	7
Very hot	450	230	8
Very, very hot	475	240	9

SUGAR BOILING TEMPERATURES

	F°	C°
Soft ball	237	114
Hard ball	247	119
Soft crack	280	140
Hard crack	310	154
Caramel	340	171

(Table2)

INDEX

NOTES